SECRET LIFE OF BEER

LEGENDS, LORE & LITTLE-KNOWN FACTS

ALAN D. EAMES
The Beer King

A Storey Publishing Book

STOREY

Storey Communications, Inc.

The mission of Storey Communications is to serve our customers by publishing practical information that encourages personal independence in harmony with the environment.

Compiled and edited by Christine P. Rhodes
    and Deborah L. Balmuth
Design and production by Greg Imhoff
Photograph on page 19 by Nicolas Whitman

Cover and interior illustrations on pages 1, 23, 27, 28, 37, 38, 42, 44, 63, 91, 92, 111, 115,127, 149, 169, 173 174 by Greg Imhoff

Printed in Canada by Interglobe, Inc.
First Printing, August 1995

Library of Congress Cataloging-in-Publication Data

Eames, Alan, 1947–
    Secret life of beer : legends, lore, and little-known facts / Alan Eames.
                p.   cm.
        "A Storey Publishing book."
        Includes index.
        ISBN 0-88266-807-2 (pbk.)
        1. Beer—History. I. Title.
TP577.E22   1995
641.2'3—dc20

95-11077
CIP

TABLE OF CONTENTS

Chapter 1 — **Words from the Beer King** 1

Chapter 2 — **Beer Is Born** 13

Chapter 3 — **Goddesses, Myth & Beer's Beginnings** 27

Chapter 4 — **Beer around the World** 37

Chapter 5 — **Saintly Suds** 63

Chapter 6 — **Beer of the Dead — Legends & Lore** 75

Chapter 7 — **Beer, Poetry & Song** 91

Chapter 8 — **Beer Is Good for You, Beer Is Bad for You** 111

Chapter 9 — **Advice on Beer Drinking** 127

Chapter 10 — **Temperance & Prohibition** 149

Chapter 11 — **Beer in Movies, Books, & Popular Culture** 173

Mankind: *The animal that*
fears the future and
desires
fermented beverages.

Anthelme Brillat-Savarin (1755–1826)

CHAPTER ONE

WORDS FROM THE BEER KING

Bes, the ancient Egyptian god/goddess of childbirth, was also known for his/her fondness for beer. Often portrayed as a dwarf with no clear gender distinction, Bes's spiritual association with brewing was second only to that of the goddess Hathor.

huddled *in the corner of a mud hut, I watched three Quechua crones bustle about the boiling beer pots. It was now long past midnight. Like the witches in Macbeth, the brewsters hovered over the brew-kettles exhorting the corn goddess, Mamasara, to work her magic into the chicha. With no electricity, this hovel was eerie, candle-lit, foul-smelling, and smokey, with dripping, bleeding, eviscerated animal corpses hung from the rafters. Herds of guinea pigs scuttled about, rat-like, awaiting their turn on the spit. The entire room was filled with bubbling beer cauldrons, like some dark medieval nightmare. Sick and exhausted, I asked myself if this expedition would count against my time in hell. What could I have been thinking? Oh yes, I'm here for the beer, the secret life of beer.*

Watching the old women brewing, I pondered the many ancient goddesses other brewsters had venerated throughout the ages. I asked these Indians, "Do men ever make the beer?" My question was met with gales of raucous laughter. The women howled. Bent over in hilarity, one replied, "Men can't brew! Chicha made by men only makes gas in the belly. You are a funny man, beer is woman's work."

Ancient Egypt; Reign
of Ramses II
19th Dynasty, 1350 B.C.

On a warm seacoast afternoon of my fourteenth summer, I fell in love with beer. The tiny, six-ounce, jewel-green glass bottles held a strong, bitter, spruce forest taste that moved me. My life changed forever. My fate was sealed. That first soft kiss of malt and hops against my lips was my first step into a world I couldn't imagine then, a journey that would take me, beer glass in hand, to some of the least travelled, most remote places on earth. From desert tombs to jungle tribes, I was always in quest of the spirit and soul of beer, the secret life and true meaning of beer. With the passing years, beer would reveal herself to me as a sacramental drink. Beer is a gift from the goddesses, a soothing balm given our species to bring joy and comfort in compensation for the curse of self-aware-ness, the awful realization of our mortality. Beer — the nourisher and the liquid bread, inspirer of song and story, tribal tale-teller, mother and father of democracy — its domestication led to civilization itself. Beer is the stuff of our species and is in our very blood and bones.

That Osiris founded there the dynasty of the Beer Kings.

PHAROAH'S CHARTER, CIRCA 2300 B.C.

Anglo-Saxon Beer Cups

I have come to sincerely believe that God did so love the world He/She bestowed upon women the secrets of beer making, a drink allowing His/Her children to share in the divine, joyous, and eternal, through tribal beer-drinking celebrations. Implicit in this gift was a test, a trial, a right of passage, a benchmark for social conduct, and a platform for politics among ancient and modern hunter-gatherers. I discovered that ancestral women maintained power and status in a male dominated society through their skills as brewsters.

Our world has seen two decades of renewed interest in beer, but, for all the new beer enthusiasm, little has been said in service of beer's role in the history of mankind. Rather, beer has been thrust into the rarified

Collection Reflection

Linger here and live the past
of armored storybooks amassed.
Hear the tales of hunt and chase
that brought them to this resting place.
Each was once a frosty well
that time has made a rusty shell
with messages inscribed upon
that give a glimpse of time that's gone.
Drained of all fermented brews
they're filled with only secret clues
of lives they touched with liquid gold
and hidden tales ne'er to be told.
So ponder this peculiar sight
partake of lager, dark or light
and muse upon these iron tombs
embodied in the Beer Can Room.

CARRIE NATION (1846–1911),
AX GRINDINGS

realms of the wine snob. A sad business, indeed. In truth, beer is the most democratic and most feminine of all beverages. The gentrification of brew cares little for the exquisite, rich tapestry of our 10,000-year-old reliance and love for this staff of life. This book will retell the long forgotten tales, lore, and legends of beer through interesting quotes, dating back to 3,000 B.C.

We have much to learn from the ancients, as well as from those who dwell at the ends of the world. Through their eyes, we better understand the importance of beer to a free and healthy society, and, thus, we lend beer the respect it so well deserves. Mankind's joy and saviour, a true gift of the gods, and, above all else, a drink with a sense of humor — this is Beer.

Whoever makes a poor beer is transferred to the dung-hill.

EDICT, CITY OF DANZIG, 11TH CENTURY

A Beer Drinker's Companion

Ale is rightly called nappy, for it will set a nap upon a man's threadbare eyes when he is sleepy. It is called merry-go-downe, for it slides

"Ale is rightly called nappy ..."

Scene in a Munich hofbrau house. Patrons are rinsing used mugs in a trough before taking them to the bar to be refilled.

down merrily. It is fragrant to the scent; it is most pleasant to the taste; the following and … the verdant smile of it is delightful to the sight; it is touching or feeling to the brain and heart; and to please the senses all, it provokes men to singing and mirth … The taking of it doth comfort the heavy and troubled mind … it is the warmest lining of a naked man's coat; it satiates and assuages hunger and cold; with a toast it is the poor man's comfort; the … plowman's most esteemed purchase; it is the tinker's treasure, the peddlar's jewel, the beggar's joy, and the prisoner's loving nurse; it will whet the witt … sharp … it will set a bashful suitor wooing; it heats the chilled blood of the aged; it will cause a man to speak past his owne … understanding; it sets an edge upon logic … it is a friend to the muses; it inspires the poor poet … it makes the balladmaker rime beyond reason … it puts eloquence into the oratour, it will make the philosopher talk profoundly, the scholar learnedly, and the lawyer … feelingly … It is a great friend to the truth … it is an emblem of justice … it will put courage into a coward … it is a seal to a bargain;

Gimme a pigfoot and a bottle of beer.

BESSE SMITH
(1894-1937),
AMERICAN BLUES SINGER

the physician will commend it; the lawyer will defend it; it hurts nor kills any but those who abuse it ... beyond bearing and ... it is the nourisher of mankind.

JOHN TAYLOR, 1580–1653

When the chill northeast wind blows,
And winter tells a heavy tale,
When pyes and dawes and doobes and crowes
Do sit and curse the frostes and snowes,
Then give me ALE.

16TH CENTURY ENGLISH VERSE

Kindly observe the tankard of beer I offer you. This bock was not made simply to drink. It was made to speak to you. And if you, with your tankard of beer, could learn the dialogue, you would discover that in your tankard lives a milky way of tiny bubbles. And inside each bubble, there exists an idea that is waiting to be discovered. Each one of these ideas can make you grand and large and fortunate if you so desire to learn to talk with beer.

M. BELLOT

... he would go for a ride on the Third Avenue "E." It would please him to see the four enormous, beautifully polished copper kettles in the windows of Ruppert's brewery, and it would please him to smell the wet hops, a lovely smell that blew into the car as it rattled past.

JOSEPH MITCHELL, THE LOST WEEKEND

The wonderful love of a beautiful young maid ...
The love of a staunch true man,
The love of a baby unafraid,
All have existed since time began.

But the greatest love — the love of all loves,
Even greater than that of a mother ...
Is the tender, passionate, undying love,
of one beer-drunken slob for another.

ANONYMOUS

The English hop plant is a species of morning glory, several varieties of which contain hallucinogenic properties.

... Man's first civilization
gave *great place* to

intoxication.

Long before there was *decadence*
or **world-weariness**, men and women
wanted to *change their response*
to *the planet* on which they had evolved to
self-consciousness.

Jacquetta Hawkes, *The First Great Civilizations*

CHAPTER TWO

BEER IS BORN

he ancient legends tell how the goddess took pity on the miserable plight of humanity and so loved her daughters that she bestowed the gift of beer to their sole keeping. It is almost a universal human belief that beer did come into the world so that the sons and daughters of men might celebrate possessed by the spirit of the earth mother and forget the sorrows of death with the barley cup of forgetfulness that gladdens hearts in song and rejoicing.

All human cultures, however separated by time and geographical distance, tell much the same tales or myths in explanation of how things in our world came to be. Virtually every culture, for example, has some variation of the story of Pandora's box. For the ancient Greeks, Pandora was charged with guarding the box of the gods having been warned to never open the casket. Her basic curiosity succumbed, unleashing forever disease, famine, death, and all other horrors and sorrows upon humanity. The end of this tale has it that Pandora found one item left in the box ... a gift to mankind. At the bottom of Pandora's box remained hope. And hope was all that was left to a suffering species. In the folktales of tribal Africa, a *black Pandora repeats her Greek sister's rash act except the African makes a different discovery remaining in the casket. Not hope ... but rather, a gourd of beer.*

Long before the bearded patriarchal male gods, there was the goddess — feminine spirit of birth and fertility. The earth mother. Twenty thousand years ago, it was a goddess who gave life and abundance and it was the goddess who, out of a mother's love and pity for her fallen children, gave the gift of brew to the women of mankind. The cup of bliss, the gourd of temporary forgetfulness was filled with beer.

Ten, twenty, perhaps fifty thousand years ago under a tropic sky a woman hunter-gatherer with a gourd of grain was caught in a torrential downpour. Fleeing the lightning and thunder, the woman left the drenched seeds behind as she scurried for cover. The sun reappeared as ambient yeast infected the bowl of abandoned, fermenting gruel. Bubbling and sudsing, the world's first brew waited for perhaps another woman to come along and spy the concoction. A curious sip followed by a grunt of pleasure at the tart taste followed

by a deeper swig. Soon a strange sensation took hold of the woman. Dizzy, lightheaded feelings gave way to drunkenness — and beer was born.

In all ancient societies, in the religious mythologies of all ancient cultures, beer was a gift to women from a goddess, never a male god, and women remained bonded in complex religious relationships with feminine dieties who blessed the brew vessels.

No children without sex — no drunkenness without beer.

ANCIENT SUMERIAN PROVERB

THE BEGINNINGS OF THE ENJOYMENT OF BEER

For early mankind, the mood-altering properties of beer were supernatural. The new-found state of intoxication was considered divine. Beer, it was thought, must contain a spirit or god, since the drinking of the liquid so possessed the spirit of the drinker. This newly discovered delight was so inspirational that early mankind decided never to be without it.

Brewsters quickly became priestesses and without beer, no one could commune with the goddess. Women oversaw the collective drinking of beer acting as barmaids and bouncers enforcing rules of conduct while ensuring men didn't injure themselves. Beer-drunken elder men became storytellers reciting the tribal tales and histories. When the elders were in their cups, the women would awaken the children to sit and listen around the fires and in this regard beer became the single most important aspect in learning among pre-literate cultures. Beer bouts were the site of the first schools of higher learning before reading and writing and all tribal wisdom was passed from one generation to the next over a pot of beer.

Some anthropologists suggest ceramics, such as clay pots and vessels, were created for the sole purpose of fermenting and storing beer. These primordial beer-makers could not have known the nutritious value in this mind-altering liquid. Beer was a valuable dietary boost at a time when wandering the land, eating whatever one could catch or gather, was a full-time, all-consuming, daily routine. The process of fermentation increases fourfold the vitamin and mineral content of

For we could not now take time for further search (to land our ship), our victuals being much spent, especially our beer.

LOG, THE MAYFLOWER

plain seeds or grains. Ambient yeast adds additional and substantial levels of protein and vitamins B and C. In nature, when rainwater meets grain, the seeds begin to sprout. Sprouting causes a natural conversion of starch into fermentable sugar. With time, women dis-covered that beer could be brewed stronger and faster if the cereals were chewed before adding them to water, because the enzyme pytalin (found in saliva) converts cereal starch to fermentable sugar.

I know Bacchus, the god of wine, for he smells of nectar; but all I know of the god of beer is that he smells of the billy goat.

Emperor Julian the Apostate, 361 a.d.

By adding the chewed mash to the beer pot, higher sugar levels created more bang to the gourd full of the local Stone-Age beer. Honey, combs and all, was an additional source of fermentable sugar. This, the oldest method of beer making, is still practiced in remote areas throughout the world.

At a time before bread baking, beer was a non-perishable food. Protected by alcohol, beer had a palatability lasting far longer than any other foodstuff. A vitamin-rich porridge, beer, used daily, is reported to have increased health and longevity, and reduced disease and malnutrition. Additionally, the self-medicating properties of alcohol-rich beer eased the stresses and tensions of day-to-day life in a hostile world. As time passed, those who drank deeply and daily thrived as the search continued for new sources of grain to make beer. It was this appetite for beer-making material that may have led to crop cultivation, settlements, and agriculture.

Ten thousand years ago barley was domesticated and worshipped as a God in the highlands of the southern Levant. Thus, beer was the driving force that led nomadic mankind into village life. With the creation of writing — stylus on wet clay tablet — beer, its history and mystery, became a large part of ancient man's literary repertoire.

I feel wonderful drinking beer; in a blissful mood with joy in my heart and a happy liver.

SUMERIAN POET, CIRCA 3000 B.C.

These words were penned at a time when goddesses, not gods, were firmly established as the protectors and providers of beer. Ama-Gestin, the Earth Mother, and Ninkasi, the lady who fills the mouth, were the goddesses of beer in the ancient world.

The fermenting vat, which makes a pleasant sound, you place as it should be above the great collector vat. Ninkasi, you are the one who pours out the filtered beer, like the onrush of the Tigris and Euphrates.

SUMERIAN PROVERB

The women of ancient Sumeria brewed and sold beer, and ran taverns under the spiritual protection of

Siduri, goddess of the brewery and patroness of wisdom. The dominance of women in the brewing arts appears time and again in cuneiform poem and prayer.

May Ninkasi live with you — let her pour your beer everlasting.

My sister, your grain — its beer is tasty, my comfort.

Pre-**Columbian beer** pot, from the chimu people of Peru

Sabtiem, women brewsters and tavern keepers, were the only tradespeople of their era with private deities who spiritually guided the making of a bewildering number of beers. "Black and White Beer," "Beer of Two Parts," "Beer from the World Below," "Beer of Sacrifice," "Supper Beer," "Horned Beer," "Wheat Beer," and the apparently foamy "Beer With a Head."

For our food, I slaughtered sheep and oxen, day by day; With beer, oil and water, I filled large jars.

ATRAHASIS, ANCIENT SUMERIAN FOLK HERO

Among the myths of Sumeria was the precursor of the Christian tale of Noah and the flood. The Noah of

LEGEND

WHEN BEER TRANSCENDED THE MATERIAL WORLD

Beer shops, called Bit Sikari, and taverns were common in Sumerian cities and villages. As drunkenness was a spiritual state, beery transactions were not to be sullied by the exchange of money. In the Code of Hammurabi the sale of beer for silver or gold was forbidden.

If a beer seller do not receive barley as the price of beer, but if she receive money ... or make the beer measure smaller than the barley measure received, they (the judges) shall throw her (the brewster) into the water.

CODE OF HAMMURABI
1500-2000 B.C.

Sumeria was Atrahasis, who brought beer aboard his ark when told by God that mankind was to be drowned for being too noisy.

Drink beer the custom of the land. Beer he drank — seven goblets. His spirit was loosened. He became hilarious. His heart was glad and his face shone.

EPIC OF GILGAMESH, THE OLDEST NARRATIVE TALE,
CIRCA 3000 B.C.

Archaeological sites throughout the Tigris-Euphrates region have yielded thousands of cuneiform tablets containing recipes for, and prayers in praise of, beer. "Kassi — black beer," "Kassag — fine black beer," "Kassagasaan — finest premium beer," and "Kassig — red beer" were not only savored as beverages, but also formed the basis for most medicinal remedies for ailments, from scorpion stings to heart conditions.

Every human culture that enjoyed beer seems to have been balanced by a vocal minority that viewed malt beverages as a threat to public morals. Cuneiform tablets cautioned the young.

Oh Lord thou shalt not enter the beer shop!

The beer drunkard shall soak your gown with vomit.

CUNEIFORM TABLETS FROM
THE TIGRIS-EUPHRATES REGION

Other social sanctions prohibited high priestesses from loitering in beer halls under penalty of death by burning. Despite Draconian restrictions for the few, beer endured as a joyful part of life. Drinking songs, sung by all classes, reflect the happiness provided by time out in the beer halls.

The Gakkul vat, the Gakkul vat,
  [fermenting vessel]
The Gakkul, the Lamsare vat,

The Gakkul vat, which makes the liver happy,

The Lamsare vat, which rejoices the heart,

The Urgurbal jar, a good thing in the house,

The Sagub jar, which is filled with beer . . .

The beautiful vessels are ready on their stands!

SONG FROM ANCIENT SUMERIA

While priestesses were forced to drink in secret, the use of attractive bare-breasted women, for the purpose of advertising beer brands and beer shops, was coming into vogue. Carved in high relief, images of curvaceous barmaids invited patrons to sample the delights of beer, and sometimes brothel.

Drink Ebla — the beer with the heart of a lion.

CUNEIFORM TABLET FROM THE TIGRIS-EUPHRATES REGION,
PERHAPS THE OLDEST BEER ADVERTISEMENT

The combination of sexuality and beer, in the form of advertising, lured the tired and thirsty into the cool dark interior of the local beer shop, while beginning a trend that would survive the rise and fall of many civilizations.

Who fed you on the food of the god?

Who gave you beer to drink, fit for kings . . .

Let sweet beer flow through thy straw,

Their bodies swell as they drink . . .

EPIC OF GILGAMESH

Let a neat housewife ...
have the handling of **good ingredients** —
sweet malt and good water —
and **you shall see** *and will* **say**
there **is** *an*

art

in **brewing.**

Dr. Cyril Folkingham, 1623

CHAPTER THREE

GODDESSES, MYTH & BEER'S Beginnings

For the Egyptians of Pharaoh, the goddess Hathor, while trying to destroy mankind, inadvertently invented beer. Hathor survived the entire dynastic ages as Queen of Drunkenness, dance, and inventress of beer. The ancient Egyptians were obsessed with beer — it anointed the newborn baby, was minimum wage for a day's work, and went into the tomb with the dead. The Nile dwellers even wrote the word 'food' as a loaf of bread and a pitcher of beer. Non-alcoholic beers also came from old Egypt. The daughters of Hathor would brew a potent beer that was taken into the temple and heated over fire, the alcohol or `spirit' of the beer rising to heaven and making the goddess quite drunk. The remaining, now non-alcoholic brew was sold to the public, the proceeds going in support of the temple.

The best and brounest ale that brewsters sellen.

ROBERT LONGLANDE,
VISION OF PIERS PLOWMAN, 1377

The ancient Finnish people preserved their accounts of the creation of the world in a song and story cycle known collectively as the "Kalevala."

hOW hAThOR BECAME the chIEF GODDESS Of BEER

A time came when the Sun God Re lost his divine patience with mankind. Re saw his temples neglected, his subjects fornicating, fighting, lying, stealing, and worse. Deciding to punish his children, Re assigned the task to a goddess, women being so much better at enforcement than men. Hathor was assigned three days in which to complete her chastisement, while Re turned his divine attention to other things. Hathor took the form of a leopardess and descended to Earth.

The First Day

At the end of the first day of punishment, Re looked to see how Hathor was doing. To his horror, Re saw the streets of Egypt running red with blood. A handful of humans survived, huddled in corners of flattened houses. Re thought to himself, "This is awful. There will be no one left to worship me." Having given Hathor three days of divine duty, Re could not now stop her. After pondering the situation that night, taking the form of a baboon Re went to Earth with the job of throwing sweet dates and barley into the human blood that covered the land.

The Second Day

The second day dawned. The sun arose and the divine mixture of blood, barley, and dates fermented. Beer was

continued on next page

ḣATḣOR'S TALE – continued

born. In her leopard form, Hathor awoke planning to hunt the few remaining Egyptians, but instead she smelled the odor of beer. Halted at the river of beer, she tentatively lapped at the brew. She found the beer so pleasing that she drank, and drank herself into a stupor, staggering off under a date palm, where she drunkenly snored for two days and nights. Upon awakening, the goddess found her time was up. Beer was created, the human species was saved, and Hathor became Chief Goddess of Beer.

*"We soothe your majesty daily
(with offerings of beer),*

*Your heart rejoices when you hear
our song.*

*Our hearts exult at a glance of your
majesty.*

You are queen of the wreath

The queen of dance

The queen of drunkenness without end."

Historians date the beginnings of these poems and legends to as early as 1000 B.C.

According to the "Kalevala," beer was born through the efforts of three women preparing for a wedding feast: Osmotar, Kapo, and Kalevatar. Their first efforts fell as flat as the brew they were trying to create. It was only when Kalevatar combined saliva from a bear's mouth with wild honey that the beer foamed and the gift of ale came into the world.

The Birth of Beer

Whence indeed will come the liquor,
Who will brew me beer from barley.

I cannot comprehend the malting
Never have I learned the secret,
Nor the origin of brewing.

Spake an old woman from her corner:
Beer arises from the barley.
Comes from barley, hops and water.

Hop-vine was the son of Remu,
Small the seed in earth was planted.

There arose the hop-vine,
Clinging to the rocks and alders.

Man of good-luck sowed the barley
And the barley grew and flourished,
Grew and spread in rich abundance.

This the language of the trio:
  (barley, hops, and water)
Let us join our triple forces,
Little use in working singly,
Better we should toil together.
Osmotar, brewer of the drink

On the fire she sets the caldron,
Boils the barley, hops, and water.
Poured it into birch-wood barrels,
Into hogsheads made of oak.

But Osmotar could not generate the ferment.
Thinking long, thus she spake:

What will bring the effervescence,
Who will add the needed factor,
That the beer may foam and sparkle,

May ferment and be delightful?

Kalevatar, maiden, gave the squirrel directions:
Bring me ripe cones from the fir-tree,
From the pine-tree bring me seedlings.

The virgin Kapo took the cones selected,
Laid them in the beer for ferment,
But it brought no effervescence,
And the beer was cold and lifeless.

Kalevatar told a marten:
Haste thou whither I may send thee,
To the bear-dens of the mountain,
To the grottoes of the growler,
Gather yeast upon thy fingers,
Gather foam from the lips of anger,
From the lips of bears in battle.
Bring it to the hands of Osmotar.
Then the bee brought honey back to Kapo.
Osmotar placed the honey in the liquor
And the wedding-beer fermented;
Rose the live beer upward, upward,
From the bottom of the vessels,

Upward in the tubs of birch-wood,
Foaming higher, higher, higher,
Till it touched the oaken handles,

Overflowing all the caldrons;
To the ground it foamed and sparkled,
Sank away in sand and gravel.
Osmotar, the beer maker,
Spake these words in sadness:
Woe is me ... badly I have brewed the beer.
The beer was brewed not in wisdom,
And will not live within its vessels.
From a tree-top spake a robin:
Do not grieve; thy beer is good,
Put it into oaken vessels,
Into strong and willing barrels
Firmly bound with hoops and copper.

Thus was brewed the beer of Northland,
At the hands of Osmotar;
This the origin of brewing.
Great indeed the reputation of the ancient beer —
Said to make the feeble hardy,

Famed to dry the tears of women,
Famed to cheer the broken-hearted,
Make the timid brave and mighty,
Fill the heart with joy and gladness,
Fill the mind with wisdom,
Fill the tongue with ancient legends,
Only makes the fool more foolish.

KALEVALA, RUNE #20,
TRANSLATED FROM PETER BORNE MISSZA'S 1578 EDITION

Beer drinkin' don't do half the harm as love makin'.

ANCIENT WISDOM

In hidden, remote places around the world from the jungles of South America to the steppes of Asia, women still hold close the arts of brewing. Praying to their ancient goddesses, the women of non-technological societies continue to pass down to their daughters the secrets of beer. The old ways have not gone but soon will be. Chanting, praying, singing inside smokey huts and hovels, women brew in the darkness under the influence of their own particular goddess while outside the men gather patiently. As the men gossip in the night, they are happy. The world may have passed them by, they may have terrible, harsh lives but tomorrow, they know, there will be beer.

Do not cease to **drink beer**,
to eat, to **intoxicate** thyself,
to make **love** and
celebrate
the good days.

Egyptian saying

CHAPTER FOUR

BEER AROUND THE WORLD

or Egyptians, beer drinking was something gods and goddesses did daily. The libation cup — the ritual cup of milk, honey, wine, or, most often, beer — would be poured over the statue of the god. The gods loved beer.

And thou shalt give to me health, life, long existence, and a prolonged reign; endurance to my every member, sight to my eyes, hearing to my ears, pleasure to my heart daily. And thou shalt give to me to eat until I am satisfied, and thou shalt give to me beer until I am drunk. And thou shalt establish my issue as kings, forever and ever.

RAMSES IV, CIRCA 1200 B.C.

Take fine, clean barley and moisten it for one day; then draw it off and lay it up on a windless place until morning ... again wet it and dry it ... until shredded ... and rub it until it falls apart. Next, grind it and make it into loaves ... just like bread, and cook it rather raw, and when the loaves rise, dissolve sweet water and strain through a sieve.

ZOSIMUS, 5TH CENTURY CHEMIST,
DESCRIBING EGYPTIAN BREWING PROCESS

Over a large fermenting vessel, these half-baked loaves were mashed and crumbled; forced through the bottom of a woven reed basket — the mixed liquid falling into the beer jar below. These clay jars, many larger than a man in size, were covered on the outside with pitch to be airtight. When filled with beer, the fermenting jar or 'hat', was then stoppered with a plug of Nile mud and lagering began.

Every household, rich or poor, brewed beer. Additionally, there were many huge commercial breweries throughout the country. Toward the end of the reign of the Pharaohs, records tell of the firm of Paison and Senthous that paid a fortune in excise taxes on the thousands of gallons of beer they brewed and sold. For the average family, the household brewery was located in the part of the kitchen called the "pure." Most often women were responsible for brewing and selling beer; both in the home and in Egypt's many beer shops. The palace of the

Fermentation and civilization are inseparable.

JOHN CIARDI
(1916-1986)

Pharaoh provided the royal household with its own regal brews; the office of Chief Beer Inspector being responsible for quality control. Further, Pharaoh received thousands of jars of beer each year in the form of taxes and tribute from cities, provinces, and territories. Beer was money; the minimum wage of the day being two pitchers, each several gallons in size, per day's work.

They who have drunk beer … fall on their backs … for they who get drunk on other intoxicating liquors fall on all parts of their body … it is only those who get drunk on beer who fall on their backs and lie with their faces upwards.

ARISTOTLE (384–322 B.C.)

Some travellers to the land of the Nile had mixed reviews for the national beverage. Greek physician Dioskorides complained that Egyptian beer caused too frequent urination. Despite Grecian fears that beer caused leprosy, the Egyptian brew "zythos" was imported by the shipload into Mediterranean ports for use by craftsmen to soften ivory in the manufacture of jewelry.

Egyptian beers all had a degree of sweetness. Bittering agents, herbs, and the like, were not includ-

ed in the brew, but were served with the beer as a condiment. Patrons of an ancient beer shop were offered platters of dry twists of skirret, a bitter plant. The drinker placed these herbal plugs between the cheek and gum. The skirret provided a pleasant bitter flavoring as the sweet beer entered the mouth.

The Egyptians make the sweet taste of their beer palatable by adding to it pungent spices and lupine.

COLUMELLA, ROME, 1ST CENTURY A.D.

When calling at a friend's house or entering a beer shop, a visitor would be greeted by a servant carrying a small wooden corpse in a casket. Holding the gruesome icon under the guest's nose, the host would intone words to the effect of: "See here? Soon this is how you shall be. So drink deep and enjoy thyself." Formalities over, the beery evening began.

The mouth of the perfectly happy man is filled with beer.

EGYPT'S MULTI-DYNASTY SLOGAN

And give a hand to an old man filled with beer.

THE INSTRUCTION OF
AMENEMOPE,
11TH CENTURY B.C.

For Egyptians, being drunk was being spiritual. Thousands of years before Jesus, respectable Egyptians would give their children socially acceptable names like: "How Drunk is Cheops," or "How Intoxicated is Hathor."

Don't undertake to drink a whole pitcher of beer. Because if you then talk, from your mouth comes nonsense ... your drinking friends in the beer-shop stand up and say only "away with this drunkard."

PAPYRUS ANASTASI IV

The hangover, which the intoxicated Egyptians called "the pulling of the hair," was of top priority to the ancient medical community. Cabbage juice was a Pharaoh's first line of defense against beery overindulgence. For hundreds of years, the modern world has recorded the ancient Egyptian cabbage remedy with great amusement. However recent scientific research has discovered that cabbage contains chelators which are effective in neutralizing acetaldehydes, a most unpleasant byproduct of our livers' efforts to metabolize alcohol.

Pharaoh's Own

CABBAGE-TROL

Powerful Cure for
"the pulling of the hair"!

Wife, quick! Some cabbage boil, of virtuous healing, that I may rid me of this seedy feeling.

EUBULUS, ANCIENT AUTHOR (CIRCA 405–335 B.C.)

Last evening you were beer-drinking deep, so now your head aches. Go to sleep. Take some boiled cabbage and when you wake, there's end of your headache.

ATHENAEUS (2ND CENTURY)

To even dream of beer was significant enough that by the 19th Dynasty (1306 B.C.), an entire volume appeared explaining the meaning of beer-dream symbols.

When he dreams of sweet beer, he will become happy.

When he dreams of bakery beer, he will live.

When he dreams of cellar beer, he shall have security.

BEER IN CENTRAL AMERICA

In pre-Columbian Mesoamerica, the Aztecs brewed a chicha-like brew called sendecho from corn and bittered the brew with the plant tepozan. Early Spanish explorers commented on the exceptional strength of another Aztec beer-like beverage called tesguino.

The Aztecs forbade drunkenness except among those who were 52 years of age and older. In a society that enforced the death penalty for violations of the dress code, this anti-drunkenness rule was strictly observed, save for religious festivals and harvest celebrations. The Aztecs believed a drunken person was under the influence of a spirit or god, represented in the form of a rabbit — a creature considered by the Aztecs to have no sense at all. Chief among the rabbit-drunk dieties was Ometochtli. On a scale of beer drunken debauchery, 400 rabbits represented the ultimate in beery disgrace. Anyone born on the "two rabbit" day of the drink god Tepoxtecatl was believed doomed to be a hopeless drunk.

The **Aztecs** had a *less than kind opinion* of the **mental abilities** of the **rabbit**

ALE AND THE VIKINGS

*A*le was perhaps the most important item in Viking life. The name Viking means "Sea-king" and sea-kings they were. Consummate seamen and navigators, the Vikings were the terror of the 8th through 10th centuries. These Norsemen raped, burned, and pillaged their way through North Africa, Holland, England, Ireland, Wales, France, Germany, and Italy; sacking such cities as Paris, Hamburg, and Cologne.

Intrepid explorers, Vikings discovered Iceland in the year 861 and, in fact, settled the country in 874. It is believed by some that America was first explored by Viking Chief Leif Ericson in the year 1000. If true, you can bet Ericson's ships had ale on board. Since the Vikings were almost always drunk, great amounts of ale were kept in huge casks on every vessel.

Viking brew was called "Aul." The Danes adapted Aul to "Ol" and from this come the English "ale." Of Viking ale, there were at least three kinds, all un-hopped, slightly sweet, and potent. These ale types were clear ale, mild ale, and, the favorite, Welsh ale. In Ireland during the 9th century, the Vikings are said

> Drunk I was, I was over drunk.
>
> THE NORSE GOD ODIN,
> THE HAVAMAL SAGA

to have brewed ale from heather using honey for fermentable sugar and adding wormwood as a bittering agent. Also, ales brewed with oats and bayberries were not uncommon.

Norse ale was often served with garlic added as a charm to ward off evil. Likewise, many drinking horns bore "ale runes" which were inscriptions to protect against deceitful women and poisons. Rune sticks covered with magical inscriptions were thrown into ale horncups to further defeat feminine wiles.

Oel (ale)-runes thou must know, if thou wilt not that another's wife thy trust betray, if thou in her confide. On the horn must they be graven, ...

Sigrdrifumal, The Lay of Sigrdrifa

When drinking horns were in short supply, the Vikings delighted in drinking ale from the boiled skulls of enemies killed in battle. While thus engaged in gory bliss, the warriors would often bleed themselves into each other's ale-skull in a brotherhood ceremony only death could undo. Such behavior notwithstanding, Vikings were the first known people to use tablecloths of pure white linen daily. Viking eti-

quette also called for getting one's enemies dead-drunk on ale and then burning down the ale-house with passed-out foes still inside. Any pledge or statement made while drunk was legally binding and a Viking might awaken only to find that he was now someone's slave or had given away his wife or property. Bear in mind that to Norsemen, beer drunkenness was admirable and the measure of a man or woman was in one's ability to drink huge amounts of ale. Rents and taxes paid in beer and ale were called "ale-gafol" and ale tribute was exacted from all conquered tribes.

Copious drinking was viewed by the Vikings in the same way that present-day people admire championship athletics. Consider the Norse notion of the creation of the ocean tides. When the god Thor was asked by the giant Utgard-Loki if Thor would care to compete in any *feats of strength, Thor replied that he would rather compete in drinking. Utgard-Loki agreed, saying:*

From this (ale) horn it is thought to be well drunk if it is emptied in one draught, some men empty it in two, but there is no drinker so wretched that he cannot drain it in three.

In spite of Thor's vast thirst, he was unable to drain Utgard-Loki's alehorn. The next day, however, Utgard-Loki confessed to Thor that the drinking contest was rigged.

Know then, that I have deceived you with illusions … When you drank from the horn, and thought so little ale was gone, it was a great wonder, which I thought not possible. One end of the horn stood in the sea, but that you did not see. When you come to the sea-shore you will discover how much the sea has sunk by your drinking. That is now the ebb of the tide.

THOR'S ADVENTURES, THE YOUNGER EDDA

In case you wonder what all this beer-drinking did to the Norseman's health and stamina …

I have never seen people with a more developed body stature than they. They are tall as date palms, blond and ruddy ... They are the dirtiest creatures of God. They have no shame ... Each one of them has from his nails to the neck figures of things tattooed in dark green.

Ibn Fadhlan, A.D. 922

Even though drunk on ale and beer, the Vikings were the absolute terror of the civilized world. Fearless, careless killers who ushered in the Dark Ages, the Norseman travelled in a state of ale-induced berserk! In this frenzied condition, the norsemen burned most of Europe to cinders. In return they gave the world the gift of ale. Looking back in time, maybe it wasn't such a bad deal.

The Chronicles of Heather Ale

In the history of Western Civilization, no beer has aroused so much speculation and curiosity as the 'lost' Heather ale of the Picts, small, dwarfish folk who were heavily tatooed (our word "picture" comes from "pict").

About the year 250 B.C., the Greek navigator and geographer Pytheas first explored and wrote of the land that we know as Scotland — and of the fierce, independent Picts. Living in villages deep underground, these tribal people were so ferocious that even the legions of Julius Caesar could not subdue them. In the year 361 A.D., the Emperor Julian witnessed the Picts in battle and said the wild, ale-drunken tribes sounded like "the bellowing of oxen and the cawing of the raven."

Pict ale, the first beer brewed in the British Isles, became famous for its reported potency and hallucinogenic power.

While the process of heather-ale brewing was a closely guarded secret of the Pict tribes (whose chieftains were sole keepers of the recipe), it is known that Pict ale was made with the flowers and tops of specific heather plants whose blossoms were gathered, washed, and then placed in the bottom of brew vats. Wort, the liquid extract from malted grain, was then drained over and through the blooms to steep. Two parts heather to one part malt gave the resulting ale its supposed narcotic property. The specific variety of heather used was the basic secret in the brewing of this beer.

As late as the early 19th century, heather-ale brewing survived in small isolated areas of the Scottish Highlands. Sadly, the 'real stuff' died out sometime in the fourth century when Scottish King Niall led his forces to exterminate the Picts in Galloway. Commercial production of heather ale has recently resumed in Scotland. Moreover, it has been confirmed that naturally occurring ergot fungus containing LSD-like properties dwell beneath the leaves of the heather plant.

Beer in Life's Celebrations

For 10,000 years, beer has been no stranger to the celebrations of life's milestones — birth, puberty, marriage, and death. In the realm of marriage, however, beer and beer-drinking customs have survived largely unchanged. The champagne toast may be more common during today's nuptual festivities, but in ancient times beer was the beverage for bride and groom. The term bride derives from the Germanic "bruths" and the old English "bryd," both thought to come from the root word "bru," meaning to brew or cook.

In medieval times, it was customary for the parents of a betrothed couple to visit every house in the

LEGEND

ḣEATḣER ALE by Robert Louis Stevenson

From the bonny bells of heather
 They brewed a drink longsyne,
Was sweeter far than honey,
 Was stronger far than wine.
They brewed it and they drank it,
 And lay in a blessed swound
For days and days together
 In their dwelling underground.

There rose a King in Scotland,
 A fell man to his foes,
He smote the Picts in battle,
 He hunted them like roes.
Over miles of the red mountain
 He hunted as they fled,
And strewed the dwarfish bodies
 Of the dying and the dead.

Summer came in the country,
 Red was the heather bell;

But the manner of the brewing
 Was none alive to tell.
In graves that were like children's
 On many a mountain head,
The Brewsters of the Heather
 Lay numbered with the dead.

The king in the red moorland
 Rode on a summer's day;
And the bees hummed, and
the curlews
 Cried beside the way.
The king rode, and was angry,
 Black was his brow and pale,
To rule in a land of heather
 And lack the Heather Ale.

It fortuned that his vassals,
 Riding free on the heath,
Came on a stone that was fallen

And vermin hid beneath.
Rudely pucked from their hiding,
  Never a word they spoke:
A son and his aged father —
  Last of the dwarfish folk.

The king sat high on his charger,
  He looked on the little men;
And the dwarfish and swarthy couple
  Looked at the king again.
Down by the shore he had them;
  And there on the giddy brink —
'I will give you life, ye vermin,
  For the secret of the drink.'

There stood the son and father
  And they looked high and low;
The heather was red around them,
  The sea rumbled below.
And up and spoke the father,
  Shrill was his voice to hear:

'I have a word in private,
  A word for the royal ear.

'Life is dear to the aged,
  And honour a little thing;
I would gladly sell the secret,'
  Quoth the Pict to the king.
His voice was as small as a sparrow's,
  And shrill and wonderful clear:
'I would gladly sell my secret,
  Only my son I fear.

'For life is a little matter,
  And death is naught to the young;
And I dare not sell my honour
  Under the eye of my son.
Take HIM, O king, and bind him,
  And cast him far in the deep:
And it's I will tell the secret
  That I have sworn to keep.'

continued on next page

HEATHER ALE – continued

They took the son and bound him,
    Neck and heels in a thong,
And a lad took him and swung him,
    And flung him far and strong,
And the sea swallowed his body,
    Like that of a child of ten; —
And there on the cliff stood
the father,
    Last of the dwarfish men.

'True was the word I told you;
    Only my son I feared;
For I doubt the sapling courage
    That goes without the beard.
But now in vain is the torture,
    Fire shall never avail:
Here dies in my bosom
    The secret of Heather Ale.'

village, taking up a collection from the neighbors. The money was used to buy the ingredients to brew ale. Wedding ale required strength, and the belief was that weak or watered-down brew would result in an equally tepid marriage. Bad luck, indeed, to serve anything but the best.

When they come home from the church, then beginneth excesse of eatying and drinking and as much is wasted in one days as were sufficient for the two new-married folkes half a year to lyve upon.

IN THE CHRISTIAN STATE OF MATRIMONY, 1543

During the Middle Ages, the word "ale" came to mean a fest, feast, or party. Beer-drinking to excess was the rule of the time. The legally bound couple, along with friends, witnesses, and officials, walked directly to the green in front of the church. The groom's mother-in-law sold the "bride-ale" or "bridal," as it was known. Strangers, travellers, and anyone not an invited wedding guest, would pay a fixed price for each measure of brew. Guests, friends, and relations, on the other hand, would pay generously, far beyond the asking price for each beer purchased. In so doing, the bride's dowery — the proceeds of the ale sales — would increase. At the end of the drunken festivities, a handsome nest-egg collected for the newlywed couple was given to the bride and groom.

As with all too many good ideas, the "bridal" party developed into a scam where seldom a day went by without a drunken revel on the village green. Often, the bride and groom turned out to be a pair of imposters hired by some enterprising alewife from a nearby village. At other times, too much ale was

brewed resulting in ale sales that continued for days after the wedding, all of which resulted in hoards of drunks lying about the scenery. Like night follows day, laws were passed.

. . . a payne is made that no person or persons that shall brewe any weddyn-ale to sell, shall not brewe above twelve strike of mault at the most, and that the said person so married shall not keepe or have above eight messe of persons at his dinner within the burrowe: and before his brydall daye he shall keep no unlawfull games in hys house, nor out of his house on pain of 20 shilling.

Court records, Hales-Owen Borough,
Salpo County, England, circa 1598

But, hey, you only get married once, right? So on it went, wedding after wedding, decade after decade. In 1787, bridals had reached such extremes that public invitations were published in broadsides alerting the public to ale for sale.

For a woman newly married, the bridal was seldom the last special brew she would be entitled to during her married life. Lasting well into American colonial

Suspend for one day your cares and your labours,

And come to this wedding, kind friends and good neighbours.

Notice is given that the marriage of Isaac Pearson with

Frances Atkinson will be solemnized in due form in the

Parish Church of Lamplugh, Cumberland, on Tuesday next,

the 30th May after which the bride and bridegroom, will

procede to Lonefoot, where the nuptials will be celebrated

by a variety of rural entertainments.

PUBLIC BRIDAL INVITATION, 1787

times, the custom of "groaning ales" marked the next phase of a wedded woman's career. When the time of a first child's birth was known, the local alewife or mother-in-law would brew a special high-test beer for "the time of the groaning" or childbirth. During labor, the mother-to-be and the midwives would swig from the ale pot to lend all extra strength for the ordeal.

Legend has it that as soon as a woman knew that she was with child, the local brewster or the mother-to-be would prepare the best ingredients for a high-gravity *ale. Lagered for the duration of the pregnancy, the cask of special brew — loaded with fermentable sugars — would fester to perfection for seven, eight, or nine months. As soon as labor began, the groaning beer was brought into the birth chamber, and the cask was tapped by the midwife. Old records tell of washing the newborne baby with the ale. The brew was known to be pure and germ-free — a real plus at a time when water was suspect for anything more than washing your feet.*

THE GERMANS

Beer has been the life blood of the German people since the beginning of recorded history. The name "German" comes from the Celtic word "Germani" and means screamers or shouters — terms of endearment inspired by Germanic tribal battle cries.

When they do not go to war, they spend much of their time at their leisure, doing nothing, only eating, drinking and sleeping … And it is notably the bravest warriors who do nothing (but) lie prone on a bear skin. As soon as they arise from sleep, … late in the day, they bathe … take their meal … then they proceed to days and nights, without intermission, in drinking. Their drink is a liquor prepared from barley or wheat brought by fermentation.

TACITUS, ROMAN HISTORIAN, A.D. 98

Eighteen hundred years later, the German beer-drinker appears to be much the same, except for the absence of spears and animal skins on his back!

I think the **Ale-house** *is that way.*

The German begins drinking beer early in the morning … In place of coffee he takes beer which he stows away as a foundation on which to build the day's work — beer drinking. There are three things the Germans are intensely fond of: beer, music, and sauerkraut. And the principal occupation of the people — man, woman, and child — is beer drinking. German beer shops are on the corners of all the streets, they are 'round the corners, they are next door and over the way, they are on opposite sides of the streets, they are in the basements or the attics, they are at the end of every dark lane and alley, and those that are not above ground are underground; in fact, beer shops are everywhere.

HENRY RUGGLES, GERMANY WITHOUT SPECTACLES, 1883

A later account by an Englishwoman tells of beery male chauvinism coupled with a bizarre drinking ritual.

In Germany, men spend most of the evening drinking beer and smoking with their friends, while the womenfolk are by themselves ... Those who sit at the table are called Beer Persons ... Young and old drink beer, sing songs, make speeches, and in honour of one or the other they "rub a salamander." This is a curious ceremony of great antiquity. When the beer glasses are filled they are rubbed on the table; at the word of command they are raised and emptied; and again on command every man rubs his glass on the table the second time, raises it and brings it down with a crash. Anyone who brought his glass down too early or too late would spoil the salamander and be in disgrace. The moment a young German goes to the university of his choice, he puts on an absurd little cap, gets his face slashed, buys a boarhound, and devotes all his energies to drinking beer.

MRS. ALFRED SIDGWICK, HOME LIFE IN GERMANY, 1908

Since ancient times, all German holidays and festivals have been centered around beer and beer drinking. A traveller to Munich for the Oktoberfest celebration, when asking directions to the beer tents, received the immortal words: You can hear it two blocks away and smell it in three.

When King William IV of Prussia visited Dortmund, Germany, a deputation of the magistrates waited upon him, one of them bearing a salver with a large tankard filled with "Adam" (10-year-old Dortmund strong ale). When the King asked what it was, and heard that it was the celebrated beer, he said, "Very welcome; for it is extremely warm," and drained off the tankard at a draught. The members of the deputation, who were better acquainted with old Adam than the unsuspecting King, smiled at each other, for they knew what would be the result. His Majesty was unconscious for more than twenty-four hours.

CORVIN, AN AUTOBIOGRAPHY

He who drinks beer sleeps well. He who sleeps well cannot sin. He who does not sin goes to heaven. Amen.

GERMAN MONK,
NAME UNKNOWN

The best *beer*
is where the

priests

go to drink.

Anonymous, 16th century

CHAPTER FIVE

Saintly Suds

The saloon is a very spiritual place. "Ah, God love ya," my white-haired Irish bartender says to me, pocketing my lavish tip while, down the rail, a drinker mutters, "Jesus! this beer is wretched!" A mere hour before, another patron announced, "God, this is great stuff!," dipping his mug into his mug of amber brew.

It is better to think of church in the ale-house than to think of the ale-house in church.

MARTIN LUTHER (1483–1546)

Today, many saints find themselves on beer bottles through no fault of their own. The majority of these holy men and women were neither patrons of beer nor even drinkers. Most of them got on a beer label through the custom of commercial monastic brewing. During the Middle Ages, nearly every abbey brewed beer for the faithful flock within the walls. Beer was critical to good diet. But soon, the church weaseled into the business of beer, selling to the unwashed masses outside. As a logo, the abbeys used each order's patron saint to create brand recognition, even if that particular saint never touched a drop.

In our world, saints abound on scores of beers such as St. Austell's, Saint Edmund's Ale, the spiritless, non-alcoholic Saint Christopher, Saint Neots Bitter, Bishop's Tipple, and Bishop's Finger — the latter hopefully extended in blessing. Wales offers Saint David's Porter, and Scotland has Saint James Scottish Ale. France produces Saint Landelin, Saint Amant, Saint Léonard and Saint Hildegaarde. Belgium, as all lovers of fine beer know, is perhaps best known for sanctified beer brands with Saint Sixtus, Saint Bernardus Pater, Saint Benoit, Saint Hubert, Saint Idesbald, Saint Louis, Saint Amands, Saint Feuillion, and Saint Christoffel. Saint Norbert oversees the brewing of Grimbergen beers. Germany offers Saint Jacobus Bock, Saint Josef's, and Saint Thomas Brau of Nussdorf.

I cannot eat but little meat,
　My stomach is not good;
But sure I think that I can drink
　With him that wears a hood.

ANONYMOUS

The selling of bad beer is a crime against Christian love.

LAW,
THE CITY OF AUGSBURG,
13TH CENTURY

Untangling the drinking saints from the teetotallers is a task made more difficult by the practice of putting saints' names on pub and tavern signs. Most often, the signboard saint represented the patron saint of the particular trade that boozed it up inside. Many pubs, for example, bear the name Saint Crispin. While I cannot determine if Crispin was fond of the odd pint or not, he was patron saint of shoemakers and cobblers. Crispin, beheaded in A.D. 308, made shoes for the poor, resulting in his death and the old homily "cobblers and tinkers make the best ale drinkers." Saint Julian, once patron saint of travellers, was a natural for an inn sign. Saint Julian's logo was three crosses.

There hang three crosses at thy door,
Hang up thy wife and she'll make four.

> DEAN SWIFT, COMMENT TO A TAVERN KEEPER

Saint John The Baptist's Head ... Good Eating

> PUB SIGN, AS NOTED BY WILLIAM HOGARTH
> (1697–1764), ENGLISH PAINTER

> **I**t is my design to die in the brew-house; let ale be placed to my mouth when I am expiring, that when the choirs of angels come, they may say, "Be God propitious to this drinker."
>
> SAINT COLUMBANUS,
> A.D. 612

One of the first full-fledged saints of beer was Saint Columbanus, who was sent to convert the fallen to Christ. Stumbling upon a group of heathen about to sacrifice a vat of ale to the god Wodan, the fledgling Saint hollered, "Stop!" and blew on the ale cask from across the clearing. With an awful explosion, the cask blew into pieces. Explaining to the frightened pagans that good ale was wasted on the devil, Columbanus asked if any more brew was around. The unbaptized replied "yes," and more ale appeared from its hiding place. Columbanus explained that ale was the beloved of God but only when drunk in His Holy Name.

Saint Adrian is, perhaps the chief among saints of beer, being recognized as such throughout the world. Saint Adrian's day, celebrated on the 8th of September,

> **F**or when the lepers she nursed implored her for beer and there was none to be had, she changed the water which was used for the bath into an excellent beer, by the sheer strength of her blessing, and dealt it out to the thirsty in plenty.
>
> VITA SANCTAE BRIGIDAE (LIFE OF ST. BRIGID)

is occasion for much Christian beer drinking in Europe. The pre-saintly Adrian was a praetorian guard to the emperor Maximilian. Legend has it that one day, while overseeing the torturing of some Christians, Adrian became impressed with the fortitude of those being roasted. Adrian was so impressed he renounced the emperor, gave his soul to Jesus, and was promptly put to the sword in Nicomedia on 4 March A.D. 303. Adrian, historians tell us, died in his wife's arms after having his own arms and head cut off. Mrs. Adrian soon followed Adrian to those pearly gates. Just how Adrian became so associated with brewing remains unclear.

Saintly women numbered among those who liked beer, including Saint Brigid of Ireland, the abbess of Kildare (A.D. 439–521). One hot day, while working *in a colony of lepers, she found her patients to be exceedingly thirsty after their bath. To answer their pleas, with Christ's blessing she changed the bathwater into beer.*

Saint Hildegard, the abbess of Diessenberg, was an herbalist whose writings include the earliest-known references to the application of hops in brewing beer.

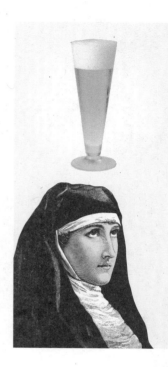

(Hops), when put in beer, stops putrification and lends longer durability.

SAINT HILDEGARD (A.D. 1098–1179) BENEDICTINE NUN

The French Bishop of Metz, also known as Saint Arnoldus, spent his holy life warning the peasants about the dangers of drinking water.

From man's sweat and God's love, beer came into the world.

SAINT ARNOLDUS

After his death, someone decided to move the bishop's bones from the churchyard to the church. The lead casket was heavy. Workmen struggled with carrying their load up a steep hill on a very hot day. As legend

has it, someone muttered in the heat, "Jesus, I wish I had a cool beer." At that moment, streams of cold ale shot out of the casket drenching those below. All had lots of drink and a new saint was discovered.

I hear many cry when deplorable excesses happen, "Would there be no barley-wine!" Oh, folly! Oh, madness! Is it the ale that causes this abuse? No. It is the intemperance of those who take evil delight in it. Cry rather, "Would to God there were no drunkenness, no luxury."

JOHN CHRYSOSTOM, GREEK SAINT, 2ND CENTURY

If but we Christians have our beer,
nothing's to fear.

SIR WILLIAM ASHBLESS

God made yeast, as well as dough,
and loves fermentation just as dearly
as he loves vegetation.

RALPH WALDO EMERSON (1803-1882)

Beer Lord's Prayer

Our barrel which is on draught
let your beer tap, its will be done.
Be in all the restaurants and pubs,
and forgive our thirst
as we forgive our waiters,
and lead us not to the police
station, but deprive us of
all the nasty teetotallers.

FOUND ON WORKERS' TOILET WALL,
BREWERY IN SLOVAKIA

LEGEND

SAINTS, FESTIVALS, AND FOOLS

"Any excuse to have a beer!" is a battle-cry heard throughout the world usually from the spouses of beer drinking males. Beer drinking under the guise of a Saint's day is nothing new. If you don't celebrate these days in your house ... give 'em a try!

Tap-Up Sunday. The Sunday before the 2nd of October was a `holy' day on which anyone and everyone could (and did) sell beer without a license. Peculiar to Guilford, England, this day was held in tribute to God's gifts; beer and barley.

Feast of Fools. Another quaint medieval custom, the Fools' Feast was held inside the church on the Feast of Saint Stephen, December 26, and the Feasts of Saint John (December 27) and the Holy Innocents (December 28). And a bizarre sight it must have been! A mock priest would conduct a mass while the ale-drunken crowd in the pews (Many with donkey-head masks) would bray back obscene responses and foul jokes. After the "mass," the ale-drunken revellers would sing and dance their way through the streets. This festival endured until the late 16th century.

Saint Monday. I still practice this holiday, which otherwise disappeared in the early 18th century. The idea was that any workman could take any Monday off as a holiday to drink beer in memory of a departed Saint, thus drinking deeply without penalty.

Saint Paul's Eve. In Wales, this was a beer fest for the wretched tin miners. Legend speaks of Saint Paul landing in Cornwall. Thus, after work miners throw stones at a pitcher full of beer until the jug is hit and broken. Then they drink. This makes sense because it is hard to hit anything with a stone when you've been drinking before taking aim.

For the Germans who follow the saints there is Munich's Saint Joseph's Day held on March 19th and the spring fest called Fruhjahrsbierfest. South Munich has Saint Leonard's Day beer fest in November.

As the world becomes, everyday, a more uncertain place, beer drinkers think of God and the Saints. One of His many gifts to suffering humanity, beer is indeed divine stuff. A joyful interlude in this vale of tears. So, next time at the bar, buy a stranger the Poculum Charitatis — the loving cup of ale. It's the Christian thing to do.

When **I** *die*
I want to **decompose**
in a **barrel** **of porter**
and **have** **it** *served in all the* **pubs** *in* **Dublin**.

I wonder,

would **they** **know** *it was me?*

J.P. Donleavy, *The Ginger Man*, 1955

BEER OF THE DEAD – LEGENDS & LORE

For the Indians of Amazonia, there were no gods, only spirits and heroes. Ten millennium ago, in the Amazon Rain Forests, complex, planned farms grew corn and manioc — the two main staples for chicha (corn) and masato (manioc) beers. In the world of the rain forest, the dead are perhaps closer to the living than anywhere else on earth. Women maintained power and status in these male-dominated, hunter-gatherer societies through their skills as beer makers, or brewsters. For these people, any social event called for a serious beer-drinking bout.

Chaco tribes drank too much beer, believing a drunken person dreams of beautiful things. Men sang and drummed through the night to hasten the fermentation of the beer. The rites of beer-making were as important as the beer itself. To the former head shrinkers of Ecuador — the Jivaro — Nunui, the Earth Mother, gave women the gift of Nihamanchi, beer.

Today, thousands of years later, women of remote places sit in a circle, chewing cereal grains; the enzyme pytalin from their saliva converting grain starches into fermentable sugars. Spitting the mash into a brew pot,

Peruvian Quechua Indians drinking **chicha** from **quart** glasses, *a custom that continues today.*

the young women (young, pretty virgins are believed to make the best brew) begin the most ancient of beer making methods. Tribes do their most heroic beer drinking in good times, not bad, and anxiety plays no part in beer orgies. Charcoal from the campfire goes into the fermenting jar; they say, to keep the spirits of the dead away from the brew. Prayer to the spirits of

> I lived from bread of black wheat, and drank from beer of white wheat.
>
> ANCIENT EGYPTIAN FUNERAL INSCRIPTION, AS CITED IN COFFIN TEXTS III, BY A. DEBUCK

the corn or manioc further strengthen beer. During the night, a circle of bows and arrows ring the beer pots to further ward away the souls of the dead.

EGYPTIAN CUSTOMS

For the Egyptians, much of this life was spent preparing for the next life. Tombs and other burials sought to ensure that the dead had ample pictorial provisions of meat, bread, and beer for the arduous journey into the afterlife. The affluent dead took entire miniature breweries, complete with tiny wooden brewers, into the darkness of the grave. In fact, as an ancient Egyptian, your last beer was seldom really your last. A step in the process of embalming was the "Liturgy of Opening the Mouth," a ceremony that took place after the mummification rites but before final entombment. The body was unwrapped and beer was poured into the mouth of the corpse — a last gargle into the great beyond.

For the wealthy, rare beers like "The Beer of Truth," were placed alongside the dead to tempt the

LEGEND

DRINKING WITH THE DEAD

In his mud-and-wattle hut in northern Nigeria, Kelembe prepared to visit his grandfather. Late for the appointment, the Koffyar man scurried about, putting gifts in a wicker basket for the long walk to grandad. Flowers, tobacco, and, most important, two large gourds of millet beer were hastily gathered as presents. Kelembe had not talked to the old man since the birth of a new daughter, and much village gossip remained to be shared with the esteemed grandparent.

Kelembe arrived at his grandfather's dwelling, a small, walled compound of crowded mounds and huts. Kelembe approached his grandfather's dwelling saying, "Grandfather, I

> **M**an's way to god
> is with beer in the hand.
>
> KOFFYAR TRIBE SAYING

am here and I brought beer, lots of the best beer!" Kelembe's grandad said nothing as the grandson came closer. (After all, the old man had been dead for 19 years.) On the tomb sat a glass with no bottom, which was set into an earthen mound. The glass received Kelembe's offering of beer, and quickly spread into a dark stain on the dry dust of the grave. Kelembe poured out his beer, and assured his ancestor that the offering was truly beer. "Taste, Grandad. This is the best brew like

continued on next page

you loved in my world, bought this morning from the village brewhouse. The women just ripened this from the new beer stock."

As Kelembe and the ghost of his grandfather drank and talked away the afternoon, the ritual sharing of beer between the living and the dead continued, as it has for thousands of years. For the Koffyar people, the dead drink nearly as often as the living. No surprise among a group whose six-day week is modeled after the six-day cycle of tribal beer brewing.

twelve gods who would sit in judgment of the deceased. The hope was to intoxicate the gods into a kinder assessment of the soul in purgatory. Other funerary beers were "Everlasting Beer" and "The Beer Which Does Not Sour" — both guaranteed to put the sternest of gods into a mood of forgiveness.

Wine made from barley … was very strong, and of delicious flavor … but the taste must be acquired.

XENOPHON, 400 B.C.

LATIN AMERICAN CUSTOMS

*L*atin America is home to many strange customs. The Conquistadors, perhaps the most brutal and cruel of Western explorers, were appalled at what they saw in the New World among the tribes of the forest: Trophy heads, skull cups, mummified heads, shrunken heads (tsantsas), skinned heads dried over smokey fires to be stretched back over the skull, stuffed corpses, skinned bodies stuffed with ashes, scalps with ears, and human stomachs dried into use for drums. Spaniards soon discovered the fine points of horror.

To the Indian mind, the dead are all around us. The pleasure of beer is still savored by those in the spirit world and the dead demand their share of suds. Tapajos, Cubeos, Arapium, and Panoans all mixed the bones of their relatives into special brews. Sometimes the bodies of the dead were buried, only to be dug up after nature had cleaned the bones. Other groups cremated the corpses, then added the ashes into beer. Still others painted the bones before powdering the remains. For the brewsters, bone ash acted as finings or clarifiers in beer,

When a dead body was laid in the grave, his beer (the priest's payment) was seven jars.

THE LAST KING OF LAGASH, ANCIENT ASSYRIA

CRIBAL DRINKING CUSCOMS

Among the forest tribes of Latin America, eating the dead enemy was called "exocannibalism," while eating the bodies of one's own relations was called "endocannibalism." Legend has it that you couldn't beat the taste of human fingers with a cool skull cup of chicha beer. The grease that spattered into the fire from a slow roasted human liver was best of all. Among the fierce Tupi-Guarani tribes, the eyes, tongue, leg and arm muscles were choice, and, by eating these parts first, according to legend, the tribes could keep the ghosts away. The Putumayo River tribes ate captives only after an eight-day beer festival where the prisoners, soon to be dinner, were kept drunk until meal time.

Jivaro women were buried with their brew pots and beer strainers all scattered around their heads. Following burial, and for at least a year after, fresh beer was placed on top of the burial mound for benefit of the spirit of the deceased. Once this ended, all was considered well unless someone in the tribe dreamed of the dead. If the dead complained of thirst in the dream, things were not peaceful with the spirits.

drawing particulate matter out of the brew, making the beer clearer. But the logic of beer of the dead was to keep the spirits of the dead within the living tribe.

Under the Cathedral church at Hereford is the greatest Charnel-house for bones that I ever saw in England. In A.D. 1650 there lived amongst those bones a poor old woman that, to help out her fire (income), did use to mix the deadmen's bones; this was thrift and poverty: but cunning alewives putt the ashes of these bones in their ale to make it intoxicating.

JOHN AUBREY (1626–1697), BRIEF LIVES

A VIKING BURIAL

*D*rinking ale all day, every day, the Norse Vikings regarded beer as the single best feature of life. This life and the next. When a Viking of rank was buried, his entire household — lesser ranked wives, slave girls, goats, pigs, chickens and favorite battle ax and all — went with him. Plied with lots of ale before having their throats slit prior to being tossed more

alive than dead onto the funeral pyre, these victims of sacrifice would go with the dead to serve him in death just as they had in life. Heaven (Valhalla) was one vast ale-house of divine proportions, with 540 doors. Inside, dead Vikings drank from limitless streams of ale that sprang from the udders of the giant goat Heidrun. Table service was provided by the statuesque Valkyries — each more blonde and beautiful than the next.

EUROPEAN CUSTOMS

*F*or hundreds of years churchyard beer-drinking was common in England and the British Isles. Those about to meet their maker left testaments in their wills, providing for ale to be brewed and given away on the date of their death. Funeral ales, celebrations at the expense of the dead and in memory of the departed, were a common feature of life that even survived to the colonies in the New World. Love of the dead, not fear, was the motivating factor behind most beer and burial practices. Evil spirits, on the other hand, were a different matter altogether. In rural

Norway, tradition held that the ale itself had a spirit. Silence ruled the brew-house. "Don't startle the ale!" the brewster would say, putting a piece of iron in the brew kettle to keep the evil dead away from the beer. Brewsters of the Northland believed that the dead went into a brewhouse to drink all they could hold, and would then spoil and sour the rest. When someone died, "Burial Ale" would be brewed. Two or three neighbors would help brew while others made the coffin and still others dug the grave.

[At a funeral service a minister is speaking of the deceased as being] "already with the One" (God). But to her, death was the end of everything. At one with the One, it didn't mean a thing beside a glass of Guinness on a sunny day.

GRAHAM GREENE, BRIGHTON ROCK, 1938

DROWNING IN BEER

Drowning in beer would certainly be a fitting end to many folks I know. Take comfort from history. Fatal immersion in beer is nothing new. The outstanding example of beery disaster occurred in London, England, on a brisk autumn day on the 16th of October in the year 1814. At the brewery of Meux and Company, of Tottenham Court Road, a 22-foot-high vat of strong ale holding the equivalent of 4,000 casks of beer lay quietly maturing within the brewhouse. The vessel, made of wood, was held together with 29 giant iron hoops. On that fateful day, a workman noticed one hoop on the brew vat had a small crack. Since each of the hoops on the vat was cast iron, weighing more than 500 pounds, the worker was not in the least concerned. An hour later, disaster struck. With a boom heard five miles away, the huge vat exploded with awful results.

A tremendous jet stream of ale shot out, crushing a smaller vessel holding an additional 2,400 barrels of brew, creating a tidal wave that smashed down the 25-foot-high, one-foot-thick brick wall of the brewery. The deluge of beer then smashed into dozens of private homes surrounding the brewhouse. Next door, a Mrs. Banfield was having tea with her four-year-old daughter when a wall of beer suddenly descended on her home. Mrs. Banfield was washed out the window and eventually marooned on a rooftop. Her little girl, however, was drowned along with a neighbor woman and child. Elsewhere, people madly scurried for the safety of upper rooms to escape the rising tide of ale.

Meanwhile, in the local pub, The Tavistock Arms, walls shook as the floor gave way, dropping a barmaid into the cellar now filling fast with runaway beer. As survivors pulled others from beneath piles of collapsed rubble and debris, crowds seized the opportunity to make the best of a bad situation by drinking from rivers of fine old ale. Eyewitnesses told of besotted mobs flinging themselves into gutters full of beer, hampering, in the process, efforts to rescue those still trapped in the ruins. More than twelve were killed,

suffocated in the crush of hundreds trying to get to a free beer. Rescue efforts continued well into the next evening as trapped neighbors called out for help from beneath tons of rubble. Homes were destroyed for a five-block radius of the brewery, an area that resembled a bomb-blasted city.

The wounded were taken to nearby Middlesex Hospital where the newly arrived injured, all reeking of beer, were admitted. Those already in the wards for illnesses unrelated to

continued on next page

DROWNING IN BEER – continued

the beer disaster soon began a ruckus which the press called a riot. Doctors and nurses were accused of holding out on what was perceived by patients to be the serving of beer elsewhere in the hospital. Pandemonium reigned.

Bodies from the disaster were collected and taken to a nearby house for identification by grieving relations. Greed ruling the day, someone began collecting admission from the curious to view the dead. So many crammed into this makeshift morgue that the floor collapsed under the sheer weight of onlookers. Many inside the building, those not already dead, perished in the collapse.

> Beer has drowned more than the sea.
>
> PABLIUS SYRUS

For weeks following the great flood of beer, the entire region was rank with the odor of stale ale, despite the efforts of local fire brigades to pump out streets and cellars. The value of beer lost by the Meux brewery (a notion considered by the press more devastating than loss of life) was placed at 15,000 pounds. The death toll reached 20, including some deaths from alcohol coma. An inquest was held to determine if anyone was liable for the catastrophe. The jury's verdict: Death by casualty.

Then a
bottle of
melodius
beer, if you please,
with a few **chromatic**
splinters in it.

A.E. Coppard, Fishmonger's Fiddle

CHAPTER SEVEN

BEER, POETRY & SONG

*V*ocal poems in celebration of beer and ale are among the oldest-known art forms. Beer, as we all know, is the drink of inspiration, and, as such, still inspires us to set the mystery of beer to music and poetry.

Among the world's earliest civilizations, the Mesopotamians and Egyptians left rich legacies of music and song — all in the key of beer, or "Hek," as the local brew was known. In fact, the ancient Egyptians authored hundreds of hymns to Hathor, the goddess of drunkenness and the inventress of beer. Most early beer songs had deep religious significance and were generally offered to the particular diety credited with revealing to mankind the mysteries of brewing.

The Middle Ages were rife with beery songs about the evils and joys of beer, most composed in the monasteries that were the taverns and breweries of the time. Throughout European history, the control and taxation of beer was the object of some of the first satirical music ever written. Musical outrage over the latest price increase in brew was one of the most common

At noon, the haymakers sit them down,

To drink from their bottles of ale nut-brown;

In summer too, when the weather is warm,

A good bottle full will do them no harm.

The lads and the lasses begin to tattle

But what would they do without this bottle.

There's never a lord, an earl or knight,

But in this bottle doth take delight;

For when he's hunting of the deer,

He oft doth wish for a bottle of beer.

Likewise the man that works in the wood,

A bottle of beer will oft do him good.

"THE ROXBURGHE BALLADS," CIRCA 1560

themes in popular music, reflecting the importance of beer in the lives of common people.

He that buys land buys many stones,
He that buys flesh buys many bones,
He that buys eggs buys many shells,
But he that buys good ale buys nothing else.

ENGLISH MEDIEVAL SONG

"Drink water," cried William; had all men
 done so,
You'd never have wanted a coachman, I trow.
They are soakers, like me, whom you load with
 reproaches,
That enable you brewers to ride in your coaches.

17TH CENTURY ENGLISH POEM

JOHN TAYLOR — THE BARD OF BEER

John Taylor, born in Gloucester, England on August 24, 1580 was the self-styled poet laureate of beer and ale. Calling himself "Great Brittaines error and the world's mirror," he was a sailor, waterman, poet, and author of satires, epigrams, anagrams, odes, elegies, and sonnets. An adventurer, saloon keeper, publisher and, for forty years, the greatest advocate of good beer and ale that ever lived, Taylor extolled the virtues of a pot of good ale in more than 100 tracts and pamphlets.

The son of a surgeon, Taylor was well educated. While working as a waterman, ferrying barges up and down the Thames River, he became the constant companion of tradesmen, bakers, brewers, cooks, craftsmen, artists, and innkeepers. This hobnobbing with the middle class made Taylor a keen observer of 17th century English life. Following a stint in the Royal Navy, the poet began in earnest his life's work: a series of eccentric journeys around England for which he solicited subscribers to support his adventures upon completion.

John Taylor

He is very facetious and diverting company, and, for stories and the lively telling of them, few could outdo him.

JOHN AUBRY, ENGLISH RURAL HISTORIAN, DESCRIBING HIS CONTEMPORARY, JOHN TAYLOR

JOHN TAYLOR'S BARROOM BET

Fearless and supremely confident, the poet John Taylor was a relentless barroom bettor. One day in a pub, Taylor made a bet that he could sail in a boat made entirely of paper from London to Queenborough, a distance of nearly 50 miles. Perhaps under the influence of his beloved ale when this bizarre bet was made, nonetheless, on a bright summer's day the former waterman (one who ferried barges up and down the Thames) launched his strange craft, built only of oiled paper, onto the Thames. While crowds of cheering rabble followed along the riverbank, Taylor rowed out, using two oars made from sticks, with a dead stockfish lashed to the end of each. John Taylor made it — wet, but undaunted — all the way to Queenborough to collect his money.

In another barroom wager, the poet bet that he could travel on foot to Prague without a shilling in his pocket; he performed this feat at age 40.

On his penniless trips, John Taylor slept outdoors on the ground between towns and villages. On occasion, particularly in his old age, the poet travelled on horseback. Upon entering a town, village or city, he would inquire as to where the best ale was to be found. Taylor believed that the best beer equalled the *best lodging. If no inn or pub were to be had, Taylor presented himself at the front door of the local big-wig in town asking for lodging for the night. Representing himself as "the Queen's Waterman" and "the King's Water-poet," Taylor explained in return for cakes and ale, he would immortalize his host in his next book.*

John Taylor's success in this gambit was nothing less than astounding. He appears to have been welcomed everywhere and, true to his word, returned kindness and hospitality with glowing written tributes to his many hosts on the quality of their table fare and ale. Taylor's writings became so well known that free food and beer were literally thrust upon the traveller wherever he went.

With washing dashing ways, and rain well sous'd
It made my mare and I glad to be hous'd
The [pub] sign was Welsh his pie-bald English Bull
I was welcome empty [broke], welcome full

But at the high and mighty Gravesend Whale [pub]
I found most potent admirable Ale
'Tis second to no drink, but Eastbourne Rug
   [strong black ale]

Put it in pot or flagon, can or jug
You'll find it is the grand Ale, and you'll grant
That 'tis Ale Paramount, Predominant
'Twas given me by a Friend; but let him end
With hanging, that loves Ale more than his friend.

JOHN TAYLOR

Concerning a pair of brewers, and a piece of justice. There was a Master Fen a brewer at Fensham, and one Master Dix a brewer at Sapham, this Dix was riding in the country amongst his customers and he called for a pot of ale as he rode by … as soon as Dix had drank, he asked who brewed that drink … the hostess said, Master Fen brewed it; well said Dix, I wager that I will give my mare but a peck of malt, and she shall piss better beer than this. These words came to Fens hearing, for which he sued Dix, and recovered twenty pounds damage, besides costs, at the assises last at Norwich 1639.

JOHN TAYLOR

Shortly before his death, John Taylor penned the first beer guide for connoisseurs. His book was a catalog of the best inns and taverns to be found in all ten shires around London with special emphasis placed on the quality of each tavern's ale. During his life, Taylor owned two saloons — one in Oxford and a second in Covent Garden. He died while serving pints at the latter, The Poets Head Inn, in December 1653.

EUROPEAN POETRY AND SONG

I was born so small and weak,
No bottle could I touch or take
Until the nurse the order spake,
"Go get that child some porter."
And so to man's estate I grew.
My medicine chart no bottles knew,
No potions, pills, or powders blue
But bottles of plain porter.
Some fear to swim the River Lee,
The Shannon, Boyle or old Liffey;
But who wouldn't chance the Irish Sea
If frothy brine were porter?
Paddy Flaherty on a binge
Travelled pubs by day and night,
But what did he drink when he got tight?
He called for pints of porter.

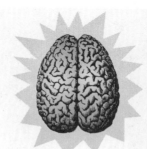

Then high and mighty town's ale I did drink there,

It made my brains to caper and career,

It was of such magnificent strong force,

To knock me in five miles twice from my horse.

JOHN TAYLOR

And now my song has come to an end.
My homeward way I soon must wend.
I'm hoping that the gods will send
Another round of porter.

Traditional Irish song

The waiter's hands that reach

To each his perfect pint of stout

His proper chop to each.

Alfred,
Lord Tennyson
(1809–1892)

They sell good beer at Haslemere
And under Guildford Hill.
At little Cowfold as I've been told
A beggar may drink his fill:
There is a good brew in Amberley too,
And by the bridge also;
But the swipes they take in at the Washington Inn
Is the very best Beer I know.

Hilaire Belloc (1870–1953)

I wish I was a brewer's horse
·For twelve months in the year,
I'd put my head where my tail should be
And suck up all the beer.

Thomas Randall, 1642

March Beer is a drink for a King,
Then let us be merry, wash sorrow away,
Beer and ale shall be drunk to-day.

17TH CENTURY ENGLISH SONG

And what this flood of deeper brown,
Which a white foam does also crown,
Less white than snow, more white than mortar?
Oh, my soul! can this be Porter?

THE DEJEUNE

The clamorous crowd is hushed with mugs of Mum
    [German beer],
Till all, tuned equal, send a general hum.

ALEXANDER POPE (1688–1744)

Oh, I have been to Ludlow fair
And left my necktie God knows where,
And carried half way home, or near,
Pints and quarts of Ludlow beer.

A.E. HOUSMAN (1859–1936)

The Old Rose and Crown

Good friends, gather 'round and I'll tell you a tale;
It's a story well-known to all lovers of ale;
For the old English pub, once a man's second
    home,
Has been decked out, by brewers, in plastic and
    chrome.

Oh, what has become of the old Rose and Crown,
The Ship, the King's Arms, and the World
    Upside-Down?
For oak, brass and leather and a pint of the best
Fade away like the sun as it sinks in the west.

The old oaken bar where the pumps filled
    your glass
Gives way to formica and tanks full of gas;
And the landlord behind, once a man of good cheer,
Will just mumble the price as he hands you
    your beer.

And where are the friends who would meet for a jar
And a good game of darts in the old public bar?

Happy the age and harmless were the days,
For then true love and amity were found,
When every village did a May-pole raise,
And Whitsun ales and May-games did abound.

ANONYMOUS

For the dartboard is gone; in its place is a thing
Where you pull on a handle and lose all your tin.

But the worst of it all's what they've done to
    the beer,
For their shandies and lager will make you
    feel queer.
For an arm and a leg they will fill up your glass
With a half-and-half mixture of ullage and gas.

So, come all you good fellows that likes to sup ale;
Let's hope for a happier end to my tale,
For there's nothing can fill a man's heart with
    more cheer
Than to sit in a pub with a pint of good beer.

WRITTEN AND PERFORMED
BY CANADIAN ARTIST IAN ROBB,
RELEASED BY FOLK-LEGACY RECORDS
— FSI–106

Pure water is the best of
gifts that man to man can bring.
But who am I that I should have
the best of anything?

Let princes revel at the pump,
let peers with ponds make free,
… beer is good enough for me.

LORD CHARLES NEAVES (1800–1876)

Beer songs have even found their way into grand opera. The Italian opera Marta, first performed in 1847, contained the following Canzone del Porter — The Porter Song.

Where else can you find you such good beer? So brown and stout and healthy, too!

The porter's health I drink to you!

Yes, hurrah the hops, and hurrah the malt, They are life's flavor and life's salt!

LYRICS FROM THE OPERA "MARTA"

You foam within our glasses, you lusty golden brew,
Whoever imbibes takes fire from you.
The young and old sing your praises,
Here's to beer, here's to cheer, here's to beer.

LYRICS FROM THE OPERA "THE BARTERED BRIDE,"
BY SMETANA, 1866

Life, alas,
Is very drear.
Up with the glass!
Down with the beer!

LOUIS UNTERMEYER
(1885–1977)

The Jug of Ale

As I was sitting one afternoon
Of a pleasant day in the month of June,
I heard a thrush sing down the vale,
And the tune he sang was "the jug of ale,"
And the tune he sang was "the jug of ale."

The white sheet bleaches on the hedge,
And it sets my wisdom teeth on edge,
When dry with telling your pedler's tale,
Your only comfort's a jug of ale,
Your only comfort's a jug of ale.

I jog along the footpath way,
For a merry heart goes all the day;
But at night, whoever may flout and rail,
I sit down with my friend the jug of ale,
With my good old friend the jug of ale.

Whether the sweet or sour of the year,
I tramp and tramp though the gallows be near.
O, while I've a shilling I will not fail
To drown my cares in a jug of ale,
Drown my cares in a jug of ale!

On the chest of a barmaid in Sale

Were tattooed the prices of ale.

And on her behind

For the sake of the blind

Was the same information in Braille.

ANONYMOUS

But now, as they say, beer bears it away,
The more is the pity, if right might prevail;
for with this same beer came up heresy here,
The old Catholic drink is a pot of good ale.

And in very deed, the hop's but a weed,
Brought over 'gainst law and here set to sale.
Would the law were renewed, and no more beer
    brewed,
But all good men betake them to a pot of good ale!

Too many, I wis, with their deaths proved this,
And therefore (if ancient records do not fail)

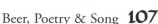

He that first brewed the hop was rewarded
  with rope,
And found his beer far more bitter than ale.

Contemporary Beer Songs

Many of the modern contributions in the realm of beer music have been in country Western music. Recently published studies by concerned Eastern liberals have revealed what we always knew — that country music leads to copious beer drinking. After an expenditure of thousands of dollars and countless hours observing beer drinkers, these researchers have at last confirmed that if you put a chorus of "Mama Hated Diesel So Bad" on the juke-box, folks just naturally swill more beer.

I'm a beer drinkin' daddy with the beer drinkin' blues ...

My honey came in, she blew her top, Lord I thought she'd never stop. Well, she's my honey and I love her dear, but she don't want me to drink beer. If you love me you'll understand, I want beer. I'm a beer drinkin' man.

"BEER DRINKIN' BLUES" BY CROWE/PYLE, CIRCA, 1940, SUNG BY ROCKY BELLFORD

I'm seein' the road that I traveled, a road paved with heartaches and tears,

I'm seein' the past that I've wasted, while watchin' the bubbles in my beer.

I think of the heart that I've broken and of the golden chances that have past me by …

The dream I once made are now empty, as empty as the bubbles in my beer.

"BUBBLES IN MY BEER" BY WALKER/DUNCAN/WILLS, CIRCA 1940, SUNG BY BOB WILLS

In rock n' roll circles singers like Jimmy Witherspoon with his landmark Drinkin' Beer have done wonders for ale sales, while simultaneously destroying the English language. New Wave or Punk Rock tunes also abound with beer-laden lyrics. Chief among these songs is the tender tune "Let's Drink Some Beer" by Gang Green.

What's made Milwaukee famous, made a loser out of me …

JERRY LEE LEWIS

We *have abolished* **sin** *by* *medicalizing it.*

Charles Sykes, *The New York Times*

CHAPTER EIGHT

BEER IS GOOD FOR YOU, BEER IS BAD FOR YOU

111

*S*cience and medicine have always had one eye cocked on any avenue of pleasure. In the grand scheme of things, the doctors and healers of the last 5,000 years seems to have respected beer as a positive component in the lives of patients.

Of course, there have always been a few voices raised against beer, even during the ancient days when beer was life itself. In Sumeria, beer was medicine for both body and soul and was routinely prescribed for a host of maladies. Perhaps the single greatest medical text of ancient times — The Papyrus Ebers — gave ancient Egyptians nearly 600 prescriptions for the entire catalog of human suffering. The key ingredient for 118 of these cures listed beer as the principal ingredient. Notwithstanding beer's unquestioned value to the people of the Nile, some Egyptian doctors insisted beer was bad, although these opinions were in the distinct minority.

His earthly abode [body] was torn and broken by beer. His Ka [spirit] escaped before it was called by God.

EGYPTIAN MEDICAL WRITING, CIRCA 2800 B.C., FIRST KNOWN DESCRIPTION OF DEATH BY ALCOHOLISM

"Don't marry a man to reform him, To God and your own self be true.

Don't link his vice to your virtue — *You'll rue it, dear girl, if you do.*"

A tasty remedy against death wilt thou take hath an onion stepped in stef [beer foam].

PAPYRUS EBERS

With Hek [beer[the Ka [spirit] is kept in balance with the liver and blood … Hek is the liquid of happy blood and body.

EGYPTIAN MEDICAL WRITING

By the time the Greeks took over in Egypt, beer, called "zythos," was blamed for causing leprosy. Another Greek complaint was that beer drinking

"There has been so much nonsense** talked about alcohol as poison … the statement that a man who takes even his bitter beer in moderation is on the high road to perdition, with ruined health thrown in, has been so often reiterated that many old women of both sexes have come to believe it. The shrieking Doctorhood have supplied apostles to the cause. To every one of these M.D.s who hold such extreme and alarmist views, the authority of equally eminent professional men could be cited in favor of moderation in all things.

W.T. MARCHANT, 1888

caused the drinker to urinate far too often than was decent for the refined Grecian way of life.

THE DANGERS OF DRINKING BEER

*I*f one can draw any lesson whatever from history, it is this: For every statement of scientific thought, there will always be an opposite and equally determined position dearly held by some few of the same scientific establishment — at least where beer and beer drinking are concerned. Today's anti-beer jargon has, blessedly, been dampened by the national anti-smoking witch-hunt. Still, each day's paper carries at least one alarmist "Beer causes whatever" headline. To put these novel notions of lingering death by beer in some perspective, here is a tiny treasury of some familiar-sounding propaganda from the past. Notice, that these dire warnings from grandpa's time could have been clipped from yesterday's paper.

Attention has been called to the large number of bartenders who have lost fingers on both hands … an employee of (a saloon) lost three fingers from his right hand, two from his left, and the physicians decided that they became rotted off by

Beer causes restlessness, irritability, tremors, chills, sweating, cramps, nausea, vomiting, and severe craving for more.

Drugs —
Close To Home,
supplement to Message
magazine, an antidrug
fundraising piece, 1991

the beer which he handled. One bartender said, "I know that it is impossible to keep a good pair of shoes behind the bar. Beer will rot leather as rapidly as acid will rot iron."

AMA QUARTERLY, 1889

Surgeon Brown ... contended that bad water and sewerage in Belfast had caused typhoid and typhus fever in that town. Mr. Mowatt replied that those who had suffered most from fever drank "Bass's bitter ale" and "Guinness' stout" and not Belfast water.

TRANSACTIONS OF SOCIAL SCIENCE CONGRESS, 1867

A brewer, who, when asked by the Doctors, "Do you know what filthy water they use in brewing?" replied, "Oh yes, I know all about it, and the more filthy the water the better. In the brewery in which I work, the pipes which draw the water from the river come in just at the place which receive the drainings from the horse stables; and there is no better beer in the world as is made from it."

AMA JOURNAL, 1837

"The boy reasons: 'Father drinks, so why can't I?' and at the first opportunity indulges —
because *Father* does.

Malt liquors may be considered wholesome, if used in moderation, by lean, nervous, cold, bloodless persons, but not by individuals of full habit.

E.B. FOOTE, M.D., 1902

If both parents are moderate drinkers, drinking but one glass of beer per day at one meal, the effect will more than quadruple the chances of miscarriage of the mother, increasing 400 percent the dangers of suffering in maternity, and will nearly double the percentage of their children that will die the first year in infancy.

DR. HOBSON, THE CONGRESSIONAL RECORD, 1914

… The increasing use of beer is worse than all the plagues of Egypt … This sodden, drooling, half-witted style of drunkenness which substitutes a stupid, boozy mass for the old-fashioned few (hard liquor drinkers), wide-awake with delirium tremens, a disease which was characterized by a certain fatal liveliness and dispatch far preferable to the wheezy and idiotic stupors of the beer guzzlers.

M.W. BLAIR, 1888

In appearance, the beer-drinker may be the picture of health, but in reality he is most incapable of resisting disease.

QUARTERLY JOURNAL OF INEBRIETY, 1850

> Beer is the drunkard's kindergarten.
>
> GARRISON KEILLOR

The beer garden recently started on this side of the river, by permission of our town board, continues to grow offensive. The rabble from the city and the country meet there and sometimes form nothing less than drunken mobs. It is not safe for women to pass along the road near this place. Bloody fights are of a daily occurrence and drunken men may be found lying around in the bushes on all sides. Wife whipping has come into vogue since the new institution was forced upon us. … What it may end in need hardly be conjectured.

BADGER STATE BANNER, 1890, AS QUOTED BY
MICHAEL LESY, WISCONSIN DEATH TRIP

THE BENEFITS OF BEER DRINKING

I would be remise in not including a few words from the defenders of brew. Even in these times of "just saying no" the odd press clip begrudgingly admits the moderate use of beer may extend life, reduce heart attacks, and otherwise make life more worth living. Most of us have always known these things, often by instinct and plain common sense, but, still, it's nice to

*watch the medical establishment forced to admit that
it could be OK to enjoy beer now and then.*

The brewery is the best drug store.

GERMAN FOLK WISDOM

There are more old drunks than old doctors.

ANONYMOUS

You doctors who more execution have done
With powders and bolus with potion and pill,
Than hangman with halter, or soldier with gun
Than miser with famine; or lawyer with quill;
To kill us the quicker, you forbid us malt liquor,
Till our bodies consume and our faces grow pale;
But mind it, what pleases, and curse all diseases
Is a comforting dose of good ale!

GEMTHORPE, 1790

Let us now speak of beer ...
By art invented,
Which makes miracles and wonders,
From one candle-stick two
Of a layman a good clerk,
Gives to a man unknown a mark,
It makes strong men creep

We don't know why beer-drinking rodents developed fewer tumors. Follow-up studies must be done.

Dr. Richard Nelson, University of Illinois, 1986

Make men shout high in the street,
Such virtues has the barley juice,
The beer made of malt,
That the headgear of a rooster
Keeps its color without vermilion.
Here this matter rests,
Let us speak of something else.

Treatise of Walter Biblesworth, Norman-French, 13th century

Upon both mind and body, then, beer exercises a gracious and salutary influence. It civilizes and sustains; it feeds and refreshes; it soothes and humours. As an influence no other drink can compare with it in humanity and companionability. It adjusts the human machine to its optimum working conditions.

Anonymous, 1934

While you merely see the disease-bearing viruses I see the benign microorganisms which by making among other things strong beers … and enable you to spend your evenings in alcoholic bliss.

Patrick McGinley, Bogmail, 1978

About 1730, Pulteney, afterwards the Earl of Bath,
lay ... sick, very dangerously, of a pleuritic feaver
... He was still alive, and was heard to mutter, in
a low voice, "Small beer, small beer!" They (the
Doctors) said, "Give him small beer or anything!"
Accordingly a great silver cup was brought, which
held two quarts of small beer. Pulteney drank off
the whole at a draught, and demanded another.

A glass of bitter beer or pale ale, taken with the principal meal of the day, does more good and less harm than any medicine the physican can prescribe.

DR. S. CARPENTER, 1750

Another cupful was administered to him, and soon after that he fell into a profuse perspiration and a profound slumber for nearly twenty-four hours. ... From that time forth he recorded wonderfully, insomuch that in a few days the physicians took leave of him.

JOHN TIMBS, 16TH CENTURY

Here John Randal lies
Who counting of his tale
Lived threescore years and ten,
Such vertue was in his ale,
    Ale as his meat,
    Ale as his drink,
    Ale did his heart revive,
    And if he could have drunk his ale
    He still had been alive.
He died January 5,
    1699

TOMBSTONE EPITAPH, GREAT WALFORD, ENGLAND

The Remedial Effects of Beer

Ale is a singular remedy against all melancholic diseases, tremor cordis, and maladies of the spleen; it is purgative and of great operation against iliaca passic, and all grippings of the small guts; it cures the stone in the bladder and kidneys and provokes urine wonderfully; it mollifies tumors and swellings in the body; and is very predominant in opening obstructions of the liver. Ale is most effectual for clearing the sight, being applied outwardly it asswageth the insufferable pain of gout, the yeast being laid hot to the part pained. It is easeful to pain in the hip called sciatica; indeed, for all defluxions and epidemic diseases whatsoever, and equal good against all contagious diseases, feavers, agues, rhumes, choughes, and all cattarres — of all sicknesses — ale doth heal.

JOHN TAYLOR (1580–1653),
THE BARD OF BEER

Of Doctors and medicines we have in plenty more than enough … what you may, for the Love of God, send is some large quantity of beer.

DISPATCH FROM THE COLONY, NEW SOUTH WALES,
1854

Beer was not made to be **moralized** about, but to **be drunk**.

Theodore Maynard

CHAPTER 9

Advice on Beer Drinking

wenty years ago in the United States, beer was the most neglected of beverages. Today beer and ale have attained chic status in our society. Neo-temperance and body-beautiful movements notwithstanding, beer in general, and microbrewed and imported beer in particular, have become fashionable. The relative merits of these beers are the center of debate as well as controversy.

In response to this rediscovery of man's oldest beverage (other than water) bookstores are home to scores of beer guides and beer books such as the world guide, the tasters guide, the great American beer guide and on and on. Those who a decade ago scorned beer as a beverage for the less than common classes, now endeavor to elevate beer to the rarified realms of those quasi-wine elitists, who debate chocolate aftertastes, the "units of bitterness," and "banana-like nose" when speaking of the most democratic of drinks: beer. Beer glasses are held aloft in hushed reverie; bubbles are studied like the ancient Greek augeers gazing at the entrails of sheep for a glimpse of the future. Beer festivals are held to determine which beer is best, not unlike the search for the holy grail.

All of this activity has left many bewildered and very intimidated. There's been an increased incidence of "fermentiphobia" — a syndrome of paralyzing, often crippling fear experienced when the unfortunate few are faced with the numbing task of having to choose a particular beer for a social gathering from dozens of selections. This is closely related to "catastrophic-doom expectation syndrome" — the fear of showing up at a gathering with the wrong brew — which is fast becoming America's most dreaded social faux pas. In other words, with awareness comes self-consciousness. We have come full circle, unable to strike a happy medium between the benign neglect of beer (as in the past) and false effetism toward beer (the present trend).

Confronted with some retched microbrew and gagging at the taste, we have been led to assume that we must somehow overcome common sense and relearn the sensibility of what constitutes "real beer taste." We have become so distanced

from good beer that we don't trust our own sensibili-
ties. A review of beer-drinking advice from the past
may help us regain some of our confidence on juding
beer and enable us to keep a perspective on the pre-
sent-day judgments of the beer effete.

As good wine needs no bush, so beer needs no
excuse. One should drink it because it is pleasing
to drink and not because it contains any specific
number of calories or because it is either good or
bad for you.

ANONYMOUS, 1934

[Beer] is an excellent wash.

GOODE QUEENE BESS

If with water you fill up your glasses,
You'll never write anything wise,
For Ale is the horse of Parnassus
Which hurries a bard to the skies.

THOMAS MOORE (1779–1852), ODES OF ANACREON,
17TH CENTURY

"What would you like to drink, sir?" he asked, holding out the wine list.

Uncle John smiled villainously up at him as he pushed away the book. "Beer. You don't imagine I am going to ruin my digestion drinking your vinegar disguised as Chateau this and Chateau that, do you? Three pints of bitter."

RUTHVEN TODD

If taking lunch at Claridges, you were to call loudly for a tankard of old ale, you would lay yourself open to three imputations. First you would lay yourself open to the imputation that you had no appreciation of good food; second that you failed to be suitably impressed by your surroundings; and third and worst and most unexpected of all, that you were addicted to genteelisms. And every one of these imputations would be unjust. With certain dishes . . . there is no drink superior to, more congenial and appropriate than, old ale.

ANONYMOUS, 1934

Life isn't all beer and skittles; but beer and skittles, or something better of the same sort, must form a good part of every Englishman's education.

THOMAS HUGHES,
TOM BROWN'S
SCHOOLDAYS, 1857

> I have fed purely upon ale; I have ate my ale, and I always sleep upon ale.
>
> GEORGE FARQUHAR (1678–1707), THE BEAUX' STRATAGEM

Hermit hoar, in solemn cell,
Wearing out life's evening gray;
Strike thy bosom, Sage! and tell
What is bliss, and which the way?
Thus I spoke, and speaking sigh'd
Scarce repress'd the starting tear,
When the hoary Sage reply'd,
"Come, my lad, and drink some beer."

SAMUEL JOHNSON (1709–1784)

Ale man, ale's the stuff to drink
For fellows whom it hurts to think:
Look into the pewter pot
To see the world as the world's not.

A.E. HOUSMAN (1859–1936)

. . . hot beer is excellent good for the keeping of the stomach in good order for concoction, and consequently good health; so it is most excellent for the quenching of thirst. For I have not known thirst since I have used hot beer; let the weather be never so hot, and my work great, yet have I not felt thirst as formerly … Cold beer is very pleasant when extreme thirst is in the stomach; but what more dangerous to the health. Many by drinking a cup of cold beer in extreme thirst, have taken a surfeit and killed themselves. Therefore we must not drink cold beer ...

HENRY OVERTON, 1641

You see those young Irishmen there, struggling like pigs at a trough to get their fill of German beer. That signifies a conquest of Teuton over Kelt ... The Kelt has come to grief heretofore ... because he lacked the right sort of a drink ...

HAROLD FREDERIC, 1896

A can of beer'd be the makin' of a guy a cold mornin' like this.

JOHN DOS PASSOS (1896-1970)

Understand he's been having a little beer. Well won't hurt him any. Won't do him any good, but there's damned little that will. Not enough alcohol in the slop they make these days to hurt a baby.

JIM THOMPSON, A SWELL-LOOKING BABE, 1954

> Beer that is not drunk had missed its vocation.
>
> MEYER BRESLAU, 1880

It has been a common observation, that both beer and ale are apt to foul, disturbed, and flat in bean season; thunder is also a spoiler of good malt liquor, to prevent the effects of which, laying a solid piece of iron on each cask has hitherto been esteemed an effectual prevention of the above injuries.

16TH CENTURY BREWERY ADVICE

The troubles of our proud and angry dust
Are from eternity, and shall not fail.
Bear them we can, and if we can we must.
Shoulder the sky, my lad, and drink your ale.

A.E. HOUSMAN (1859–1936)

For it (beer) possesses the essential quality of gulpability. Beer is more gulpable than any other beverage and consequently it ministers to the desire to drink deeply. When one is really thirsty the nibbling, quibbling, sniffing, squinting technique of the wine connoisseur becomes merely idiotic. Then is the moment of the pint tankard of bitter.

ANONYMOUS, 1934

If you have ... drunk two containers of beer and your body is not yet satisfied, fight against it. If then another would satisfy you, don't step up to the table and press yourself against it.

COUYAT-MONTET,
INSCRIPTIONS OF THE WADI HAMMAMAT #87,
ANCIENT EGYPT

Ye bishops and deacons, priests, curates, and vicars,
   When once you have tasted you'll own it is true,
That Nottingham ale is the best of all liquors;
   And who understands the good creature like you?
It expels every vapour — saves pen, ink, and paper;
   And when you're disposed from the pulpit to rail,

Thou reprobate mortal! why, dost thou not know
  Whither, after your death, all you drunkards must go?
Must go when we're dead? Why, sir, you may swear,
We shall go, one and all, where we find the best beer.

AN ANONYMOUS MINISTER, CIRCA 1880

'Twill open your throats — you may preach without notes
    When inspired with a bumper of Nottingham ale.

JOHN BLACKMAN, 1815

THE CULTURE OF BEER

I think if I had to say one thing about beer, above all others, it's that beer is a democracy. From the very earliest beginnings of human settlements and civilization, beer halls were the levelers of classes. When you walked through those swinging doors in Sumer or Babylon, you were on democratic common ground. You were able to speak to your boss or the high "muckity-mucks" on an equal basis. This was the value of the tavern or the public house — or beer gardens, what a wonderful notion!

Beer goes with the crowd to Coney Island, lodge picnics and clam bakes. It follows the races, attends prize fights and ball games. It accompanies the fisherman to the brook and awaits him in the coolness of the spring. It rides the Twentieth Century, lives at the Ritz, and greets the dusty traveller at the hot dog stand. The furtive maid opens it on the kitchen table for her sweetheart while the butler serves it to his master on a silver tray. It christens the freshman, returns the alumnus and presides at the midnight feast.

OBIE WINTERS

I saw the first sign of life since April 21 — two beer bottles. I said, I must be close.

CHRISTOPHER TRUMP, TORONTO EDUCATOR, AT PRESS CONFERENCE IN HOSPITAL IN PUYALLUP, WASHINGTON, AFTER SPENDING A WEEK LOST ON SNOW-COVERED MOUNT RAINIER BEFORE BEING SPOTTED BY NATIONAL PARK SERVICE RANGERS IN A HELICOPTER

LEGEND

Learn to enjoy it for its own sake

Ruthven Todd, a highly respected poet in England, wrote two mystery novels during the 1920s and '30s, under the pen name R.D. Campbell. The detective in these books, *Bodies in a Bookshop* and *Always a Body to Spare*, had strong opinions about beer.

"Beer," he was shouting, "varies more than any other drink and is more of a gamble. You know that a bottle of a certain wine of a certain vintage should be drinkable, but you go into a strange pub and order a pint of four-ale you got no surety that it'll be any good. The pubkeeper may not take care of his pipes, his cellar may not be the right temperature. The beer may be sour or flat or one of a million other things. Beer, I tell you, is the hell of an undependable drink. In spite of the fact that he drinks it, an Englishman knows nothing about his national drink. So far as the Englishman is concerned, his beer might be a chemical compound that started its life in a laboratory at the other end of a pump, and it often tastes as if it was. The next time you take a glass of beer, my good fellow, think of it as a drink and not as medicine. Instead of ramming it back into your stomach — a disgustin' German students' trick — try tastin' it. Yes I said try tastin' it. Don't look so damned surprised. It won't poison you and you'll learn to enjoy it for its own sake."

The Puritanical nonsense of excluding children and — therefore — to some extent women from pubs has turned these places into mere boozing shops instead of the family gathering places that they ought to be.

GEORGE ORWELL (1903-1950)

If you carry out a blindfold test . . . you'll find that the beer snob is just as much a galah as the wine snob.

CYRIL PEARL, BEER, GLORIOUS BEER, 1969

Lo! the poor toper whose untutur'd sense,

Sees bliss in ale, and can with wine dispense;

Whose head proud fancy never taught to steer,

Beyond the muddy ecstasies of beer.

GEORGE CRABBE, INEBRIETY

Beer is the cause of all the radical pot-politics that men talk over it.

OTTO VAN BISMARCK (1815-1898)

And there are few things in this life so revolting as sipped beer. But let it go down your throat "as suds go down the drain," and you will quickly realize that this is a true friend, to be admitted to your most secret counsels. Long draughts with an open throat are the secret.

MAURICE HEALY, 1940

The rolling English drunkard made the rolling English road.

G.K. CHESTERTON
(1874–1936)

I pour a round of Lowenbrau, being careful not to pour along the side but straight down so the beer can express itself, and they say, "Did you ever try Dockendorf?" It's made by the Dockendorf family from hand-pumped water in their ancient original family brewery in an unspoiled Pennsylvania village where the barley is hauled in by Amish families who use wagons with oak beds. Those oak beds give Dockendorf its famous flavor. These beer bores …

GARRISON KEILLOR, LAKE WOBEGON DAYS, 1985

When the beer bubbles, the masses forget their troubles.

THE PEOPLE'S DAILY, PEKING, CHINA, 1991

I use no porter … in my family, but such as is made in America: both these articles may now be purchased of an excellent quality.

GEORGE WASHINGTON, 1789

When I conducted a beer-rating session last year, I wrote that most American beers taste as if they were brewed through a horse. This offended

It is the general consensus of opinion that "near beer" is utterly useless as a beverage, that it affords no pleasure whatsoever and that it is a waste of time to bother with it. The consumption of six or eight bottles gives them a sense of nauseated fullness with none of the stimulated sense of well-being that the old-time beer gave after only two or three bottles.

DEPARTMENT OF WELFARE, CITY OF NEW YORK, KINGS COUNTY HOSPITAL, AUGUST 24, 1920

many people in the American beer industry, as well as patriots who thought I was being subversive in praising foreign beers. Now I must apologize. I have just read a little-known study of American beers. So I must apologize to the horse. At least with a horse, we'd know what we're getting.

MIKE ROYKO

Beer makes you feel the way you ought to feel without beer.

HENRY LAWSON

Listening to someone who brews his own beer is like listening to a religious fanatic talk about the day he saw the light.

ROSS MURRAY,
MONTREAL GAZETTE,
1991

Fill a large casserole with good baking apples, sugar, and lemon. Seal with a roll of rich pastry crust, and bake. When done, remove crust, divide into triangular pieces, and arrange around the apples in the casserole. Pour over all 1 quart hissing hot ale. Serve with spit-roasted ox, blackbird pie, or roasted boar.

WILLIAM HONE, EVERY-DAY BOOK, (1826–7)

I'm the man, the very fat man,
that waters the workers' beer.
Yes, I'm the man, the very fat man,
That waters the workers' beer.
What do I care if it makes them ill,
If it makes them horribly queer —
I've a car, a yacht, and an aeroplane,
And I waters the worker's beer.

ENGLISH DEPRESSION SONG, WRITTEN BY PADDY RYAN
FOR THE UNITY THEATRE, CIRCA 1930

I think this would be a good time for a beer.

FRANKLIN D. ROOSEVELT, 1933

Brewed a vessel of strong beer … My two large pigs, by drinking some beer grounds … got so

amazingly drunk by it, they were not able to
stand and appeared like dead things almost …
I never saw pigs so drunk in my life.

JAMES WOODFORD, DIARY OF A COUNTRY PARSON,
1758-1802

"YOU'LL NEVER MISS THE WATER"

The government that increases the price of beer
cannot last longer than the next plum harvest.

CZECHOSLOVAKIAN HOMILY

I throw a little dry malt, which is left on purpose,
on the top of the mash, with a handful of salt, to
keep the witches from it, and then cover it up.

INSTRUCTIONS FOR BREWING SCOTCH ALE, 1793

In this year, about the Feast of John the Baptist,
our ale failed.

CHURCH RECORDS, DUNSTABLE, ENGLAND, 1262

One of the roles of beer about this time [1650s]
was that of consoling those in distress or trouble.
Hugh Latimer had a goblet of spiced ale with his
supper the night before he was burned alive, while
Mary Queen of Scots, who was partial to the brown

beer of Burton-on-Trent, had supplies of this excellent brew sent to her during her long captivity at Fotheringay. It helped her to pass the days until her execution in 1587. Sir Walter Raleigh, on the morning of his execution in 1618, treated himself to a cool tankard and a soothing pipe of tobacco.

JOHN WATNEY, 1974

I'm goin 'ome to Blightly — aint I glad to 'ave
    he chance!
I'm loaded up wiv fightin', and I've 'ad my
    fill o' France; …
I've looked upon the wine that's white, and on the
    wine that's red
I've looked on cider flowin', till it fairly turned
    me 'ead;
But oh, the finest scoff will be, when all is done
    and said,
A pint o' Bass in Blighty in the mawnin'.

ROBERT W. SERVICE (1874–1958)

As for drinks, we shall have to make some beer.

FATHER LEJEUNE, CANADA, 1634

WRAPPED UP BY BEER

Beer is a light, narcotic, alcoholic beverage, which charms us into a state of gladness and soft hilarity; it protects our hearts against stings of all kinds, awaiting us in this valley of misery; it diminishes the sensitiveness of our skin to the nettles and to all the bites of the numberless, detestable human insects that hum, hiss, and hop about us. The happy mortal who has selected beer as his preferred stimulant imbeds greater griefs and joys in soft pillows; surely thus being wrapped up he will be able to travel through this stormy life with less danger. Yes, I find such a perfection of forms, such a softness and ductility of the tissue in the pale juice of barley, that I, to express its physiology with a few words, might say: "It is to us in our lifetime like a wrapper which enables our fragile nature unendangered to reach the safe port."

PAOLO MONTEGAZZA, M.D., CIRCA 1850

Everybody drank, and nobody drank moderately; the vice was common to all . . .

At social parties no gentleman ever thought of leaving the table sober; the host would have considered it a slight on his hospitality.

F.W. HACKWOOD, COMMENT ON MANNERS, 18TH CENTURY ENGLAND

(I recommend) ... bread, meat, vegetables and beer.

SOPHOCLES (CIRCA 496–406 B.C.)

Wine is but single broth, ale is meat, drink, and cloth.

16TH CENTURY ENGLISH PROVERB

*Close every **saloon**,*
every brewery; . . .

death

*to the **seller**, or **maker**, (of beer).*

General John J. Pershing (1860–1948)

CHAPTER TEN

TEMPERANCE & PROHIBITION

INSTEAD OF LOCKING UP THE MAN FOR DRINKING WOULDN'T IT BE BETTER TO —

LOCK UP THE SALOON AND LET THE MAN GO TO WORK TO SUPPORT HIS FAMILY.

*T*he American Temperance Movement was never concerned with temperate enjoyment of beer and other alcoholic beverages. An oxymoron, Temperance was a term meaning the total eradication of all alcoholic drinks and the places that served them — especially the "Devil's playground," the Saloon.

Among the body politic of today's anti-alcohol movement, three cherished themes exist which first found expression in the anti-saloon art of the American Women's Temperance organizations during the period between 1860 to 1900.

The first is the problem drinker as "victim." In temperance art, the drinker is lured, enticed, seduced, or just plain herded into becoming an alcoholic ruin — a matter of usually less than a week or ten days. All drunkards are blameless foils for the saloon, brewery or distillery interests; interests lying in wait to pounce upon the fair flower of young American manhood. This notion survives today in the Calvinistic precept of "love the sinner, hate the sin." Love the alcoholic, hate the beer, gin, or whiskey is the watchword of many a TV talk-show.

The second hallowed ideal is the vision of the long-suffering, good woman at home. Bankrupt and starving due to her once loving husband's fiendish addictions, drinking was then in popular imagination anyway, "The Good Man's Weakness." Women were thought exempt from temptations of the bar-room. It would take Prohibition in the 1920s to introduce millions of females to the pleasures of saloons and cocktails.

The third and still popular belief is that if daddy was a boozer, little Ferguson will be, too. Although the theory of genetic predisposition to alcoholism dates to the time of the Pharaohs, the concept of the DNA-doomed drunkard reached full flower during the late 19th century.

Above all, temperance art and literature foster the idea that abusive drinking is the direct result of evil seduction of the innocent by the forces of darkness, i.e., the booze industry. All drunkards are innocent of any responsibility for their plight. All alcoholics are helpless, victims.

Chief in the arsenal of weapons used by temperance ladies was to create a rumpus of such magnitude sufficient to embarrass the beer guzzler from ever showing his face inside the swinging saloon doors. Friday night saloons were invaded by scores of women — all dressed in their Sunday best — singing at the top of their lungs such old evergreens as "Nearer My God To Thee," "Lips That Touch Liquor Shall Never Touch Mine," or "Has My Darling Willy Been Here Tonight?" Such caterwauling drove all but the most hardened beer drinkers out into the night. As women were responsible for creating these disturbances — respectable women at that — police were loath to interfere by arresting the ladies for breach of peace.

I am told that you neglect your studies, have a desire for enjoyments, and go from tavern to tavern. Whoever smells of beer is repulsive to all; the smell of beer holds people at a distance, it hardens your soul … You think it proper to run down a wall and to break through the board gate; the people run away from you. You beat them until sore … Do not give the mugs a place in your heart; forget the goblets; … You sit in the hall, you are surrounded by the nymphs; you arise and act foolishly … you sit in front of the girl, you are rubbed with oil, a wreath of burrs is around your neck; you beat your stomach like a drum, you stumble, you fall upon your stomach, you are smeared with filth.

PAPYRUS SALLIER I AND PAPYRUS ANASTASI IV,
ANCIENT EGYPT

Beer has virtue only in giving its victims more of the good-natured stupidity of the idiot and less of the demoniac frenzy of the madman.

LYMAN BEECHER, 1826

It may also be said of beer drinking that there is less limitation to it than to the habitual use of other drinks. It does not produce speedy intoxication. When the drinker becomes accustomed to it, it will scarcely produce active intoxication in

THE FIRST DROP.

THE LAST DROP.

any quantity. It makes him heavy, sleepy, and stupid. Even in moderate quantities, its tendency is to dullness and sluggishness of body and mind. Beer drinkers are constant drinkers. Their capacity becomes unlimited. The swilling of the drink becomes a regular business. It has no arrest or suspension, like whiskey drinking, to admit of recuperation. The old definition of a regular beer drinker was true: — "Every morning an empty barrel, every night a barrel of beer."

H. WILLIAM BLAIR, 1888

The use of beer is especially damaging to boys …
These stimulants excite the passions, and produce
a clamoring for sensual gratification which few
boys or young men have the will-power or moral
courage to resist.

J.H. KELLOGG, M.D., 1888

The lecturer, speaking from the pulpit, produces a
phial containing what purports to be the alcohol
extracted from one pint of beer, and telling his
audience that he is going to demonstrate what an
all-devouring fiend lurks in this substance, he
orders the lights in the church to be turned out,
and then proceeds to apply a match to the alcohol, whereupon, the flame from the alcohol
extracted from one pint of beer lights up the
entire church for a period of ten minutes.

PERCY ANDREAE, 1915

Dost thou think, because thou art virtuous, there
shall be no more cakes and ale?

WILLIAM SHAKESPEARE, TWELFTH NIGHT

Blessing of your
heart, you brew
good Ale.

WILLIAM SHAKESPEARE,
THE TWO GENTLEMEN
OF VERONA

LEGEND

BALLAD OF A YOUNG MAN

There was a young man, and he came to New York

to find him-self a lucrative position befitting his talents.

And he haunted all the employment agencies, but was nearly starved to death,

When at last he got a job in a stone quarry with all the other college grad-uates.

And after work was done

they lured him into a saloon

and tempted him to drink

a glass of beer.

But he's promised his dear old Mother

that he never would imbibe,

that he'd never touch his lips to a glass

containing liquor.

They laughed at him and jeered

and they called him a cow-yard

Till at last he clutched and drained

the glass of beer.

When he seen what he had did

he dashed his glass upon the floor

and staggered out the door

with delirium tremens

And the first person that he met

was a Salvation Army lass

and with one kick he broke

her tambourine.

When she seen what he had did

She placed a mark upon his brow

with a kick that she had learned before

she was saved.

And the moral of this tale

is to shun that fatal glass

and don't go around kicking

other people's tambourines.

CIRCA 1928

"WHERE IS MY WANDERING BOY TONIGHT"

"Taking care of the Drunkards children"

Those poor old inebriates in Hinky-Dink's saloon in Chicago, they [are] excluded from the possibility of parentage and therefore they don't harm anybody but themselves. But, nevertheless, there are a certain younger class of them who are in the habit of drinking, and they are to be the parents of the next generation. In this there is ... danger where they do not have Prohibition ... where you were dealing with a stock which is already defective, a stock which is defective in itself, you can only produce defective stock from it and therefore it is better to destroy the stock entirely ... this has been advocated by a great many medical men, in the last half century or so ... we must cut off the propagation of these defectives or they will overpower us.

In order to do that, I suggest, not to kill the individual or anything of that kind, but the humane method ... the real solution to this problem would be to confine them to farms where they would be treated kindly and mercifully, in a sort of colony where they would be prevented from reproducing.

RECOMMENDATION OF DR. STOCKARD OF CORNELL UNIVERSITY AND DR. C.W. SALEEBY OF LONDON TO ESTABLISH CONCENTRATION CAMPS FOR CHRONIC BEER DRINKERS, AS PRESENTED TO THE FIFTEENTH INTERNATIONAL CONGRESS AGAINST ALCOHOLISM, WASHINGTON, D.C., 1920

The whistle of a great harvesting machine shop blows announcing the noon hour. Into a nearby saloon, sweat-streaked, soot-begrimed men came in a steady stream. The writer counted thirty-three of them, hurrying from the awful heat which an August day and the stifle of the molding room of a great foundry had inflicted on these tired sons of toil ...

Up to the rude pine bar they came, like thirsty sheep to a running stream. As the schooners of beer were handed up, not a word was heard, only

the thirsty gurgle of the cooling liquid allaying parched throats. One by one they left the bar and dropped in weariness to the rude benches and beer kegs standing about on the sawdust strewn floor, each with lunch box, dinner pail or basket in hand.

Joseph Debar, circa 1920

When the beer is in the man
Is the wisdom in the can?

OLD DUTCH SAYING

Nothing in the whole animal kingdom is viler
than a brewer when he is robbed of his drink.
The war measures [temperance] have touched the
pocketbooks of the brewers, and they are now
furious. They are foaming with rage.

MR. LARSEN-LEDET, 1920

Close every saloon, every brewery; ... death to
the seller, or maker, (of beer).

GENERAL JOHN J. PERSHING (1860–1948)

If prohibition fails to kill beer outright, amateur
home-brewing may yet finish it off.

BOB BROWN, 1932

How can I, who drink ... bitter beer every day of
my life, coolly stand up and advise hard-working
fellow-creatures to take the pledge?

W.E. GLADSTONE (1809–1898)

And when I think
upon a pot of beer.

LORD BYRON
(1788-1824),
DON JUAN

... There are 313 taverns where you (if a member of the male sex) can sit and drink a glass of beer ... It is a beer garden — a beer saloon. And if this does not satisfy you there are 801 beer stores, where you can buy beer by the bottle, case or barrel ...

MRS. SINCLAIR LEWIS,
ON THE QUEBEC TEMPERANCE SYSTEM, 1922

Three quarts a day is an average amount for a "true Bavarian" while thousands of them strain their waist-bands to accommodate eight quarts a day the year round. Though there is little of what is politely called "drunkenness" among them, the habit of beer drinking causes want, idleness, disease, squalor, vice, and crime to abound. As an outcome of this habit, a great proportion of the people are too poor to marry under their laws, and hence, fully one-half of their children are of illegitimate birth — a scandal to all pretension to civilization.

ELISAH CHENERY, M.D., 1889

Children, beware of wine, and beware of Beer as well. It is a very popular drink in America as well as in Europe, but it is dangerous, a ruinous beverage. Some say it is nutritious. How false. Liebig shows that "one must drink twenty-three barrels of it to get as much nutriment as there is in a five-pound loaf of bread." Try the bread, and shun the beer. Let this be our motto, "touch not, taste not, handle not."

REV. J.H. VINCENT, 1892

There are few acts more reprehensible than that of parents sending their children to the neighboring saloons for beer, or sadder sights than to see these little ones, who can hardly reach up to the top of the counter, buying beer, and then stopping in the street, as the writer has seen them do, to take a drink out of the pails and pitchers of beer which they were carrying home.

DOMINION CHURCH OF ENGLAND JOURNAL, 1887

Now, you watch those children. They'll drink half that beer 'fore they get home, and their mother

"This is the last time I'll ever cross this threshold— I'm going to give my boy a fair chance — you'll never get another cent from me."

will scold me for not giving a good pint, and I've given nearly a quart. I have lots of such customers, girls and boys and women form half our trade. We call it family trade. It pays our expenses. Our profits come from the drinkers at the bar. But I tell you what — half the children who come here drink. That's how drunkards are made. Their mothers and fathers send 'em for beer. They see the old folks tipple, and begin to taste the beer themselves. Few of the children who come in here for beer or ale carry a full pint home … We must sell it, however, when their parents send for it … Business is business.

INTERVIEW WITH A BARTENDER, NEW YORK HERALD,
1880

There is always upon the counter a plate of pickled codfish, or red herring cut into proper length, or pretzels covered with salt, all thirst-provoking and they actually put salt into the beer, that the desire for the pleasant liquor may be increased. Beer becomes a necessity to him before he is aware of it, and his fate is fixed. Lager-beer originally contained only three or four percent of alcohol, but it now contains ten and twelve percent. The original beer did not make drunkards fast enough … . The beer drunkard is the worst drunkard in the world, and his chains are the heaviest and strongest.

PETROLEUM V. NASBY, CIRCA 1880

In or around the year 1820, a clergyman belonging for some time to the Methodist Church, one whom I had often heard preach, cut his throat from ear to ear in my parlor in broad daylight … This man had been highly respected for piety and talents, but he fell by indulging in the moderate drinking of ale, until he became a drunkard. Remorse of conscience drove him to the horrid act. He seldom drank anything but ale.

W.K. PITTSBURGH, CIRCA 1850

… Science knows what the Germans call the Bierherz, that is the beer heart, the heart unable to accomplish its work properly as a consequence of beer intemperance.

A. HOLITSCHER, M.D., 1920

There's an empty glass
          and a fight or two,
And a fine to pay
          for an eye that's blue.

All? Why, no, there is
          half untold:
There's a heart grown sick
          and limbs grown cold;

MR. BEER BOTTLE TAKES A WALK

"How good I feel," chuckled Mr. Beer Bottle, as he stretched his funny little legs and patted his full stomach.

"A nice walk out in the fresh air would be just the thing for me. I believe I shall go over and call on Mr. Milk Bottle. I'll show him I'm just as fine a fellow as he."

Now, funny Mr. Beer Bottle hadn't gone far before he met Trit-trot, the horse.

"Good morning," said Mr. Beer Bottle in his loudest tones, "how are you?"

Trit-trot arched her brow, and lowered her fine neck to Mr. Beer Bottle's level.

"I certainly am glad to see you," Mr. Beer Bottle went on. "I was just looking for some one to drink with me."

To his surprise, Trit-trot wheeled suddenly on her hind heels and galloped away, calling back as she went, "Mr. Beer Bottle, I drink only pure, crystal water from the cool spring!"

Mr. Beer Bottle was much displeased at this, but only muttered to himself as he walked on.

Soon he met Tabby, the cat. Tabby was stealing carefully through the tall grass and was indeed surprised to see Mr. Beer Bottle. For Mr. Beer Bottle did not often go out walking alone.

"Good morning," said Mr. Beer Bottle, as he lifted his cork hat.

Catching a whiff of his breath, dainty Tabby Cat turned to go.

"Oh, do not go!" called Mr. Beer Bottle. "Come, let us drink together."

"Indeed, no," called Tabby Cat, disappearing. "I drink only fresh, white milk. Besides, sir, your breath is terrible, terrible, sir!"

"I hope Mr. Milk Bottle will be at home when I get there," he thought. "Perhaps he has been talking behind my back."

Going still farther, Mr. Beer Bottle came upon Mr. Squeaky Pig hurrying home.

"Good morning," said Mr. Beer Bottle, "you seem to be in a hurry."

"I am very thirsty," grunted Squeaky Pig.

"Fine! That is just what I wanted to hear! Come, have a drink with me."

"Indeed not! Do you think I want to be Mr. Bleary-eyed Man? Thank you, I would rather drink swill from my own trough." And Squeaky Pig was done.

Mr. Beer Bottle was dreadfully displeased to be turned down in such an insulting way.

As he walked on, he suddenly saw Mr. Fat Man sitting on a log, resting.

"Ah," thought Mr. Beer Bottle, "here is an old friend. He will surely drink with me."

continued on next page

MR. BEER BOTTLE ... – CONTINUED

"Good morning, friend," he called to Mr. Fat Man.

Mr. Fat Man gave no hearty greeting in return, but instead frowned.

"Do not call me friend," he shouted. "We are no longer friends. Once I thought we were friends. But you ruined my good name, made me a poor man, caused my dear wife to hate me, and made my little children go hungry. Go away, Mr. Beer Bottle, I never want to see you again."

Mr. Beer Bottle was very sorrowful at having lost such a good friend as Mr. Fat Man. He thoughtfully dropped down upon a stump to rest. It wasn't far to Mr. Milk Bottle's house now.

"Perhaps I *am* wrong," he thought. "Mr. Milk Bottle has always told me I had no place in the world. Dear me, what a problem life has become!"

Suddenly Mr. Beer Bottle jumped up. "I have it," he said, "I shall go home, and this very afternoon I shall make plans to win my friends back."

All the way home he chuckled to himself. "Won't Mr. Milk Bottle be surprised when he learns I am no longer Mr. Beer Bottle — because from now on I'm going to be in a health drink business."

NELLIE MILLS,
FROM THE YOUNG CRUSADER,
CIRCA 1960

"Have You a Boy to Spare?"

Care to

join

*us in a glass
of beer?*

Humphrey Bogart,
as killer Duke Mantee
in "The Petrified Forest"

CHAPTER ELEVEN

BEER IN MOVIES, BOOKS & POPULAR CULTURE

Because movies reflect the ways we look at life, it comes as no surprise that beer has often found itself in films. Early silent films abound with wonderful scenes of the beer halls and saloons our grandfathers were fortunate enough to enjoy. The appearance of a glass of beer was most often the on-screen signal that something humorous was about to happen. In this polite fiction of polite society, beer drinking on camera was an activity to be winked at as beer drinking was generally considered "the good man's weakness."

By the early nineteen-twenties and the advent of Prohibition, beer figured most often into Hollywood gangster fantasies; lurid visions of illicit breweries run by machine gun toting brewmasters and their scar-faced henchmen. Film history tells of a movie being made to combat this negative view of beer and beer drinking. The film, called "Liquid Bread," was based on a pro-beer, anti-temperance play entitled "The Passing of Hans Dippel." In the play, and possibly the film version, Mr. Dippel is an honest, hard working beer-hall keeper whose life and fortune are ruined by the hysterics and propaganda of the Prohibition movement. His saloon closed by law, and without compensation from the town for his now lost income, Dippel is bankrupt. Worse still, the honest working man is without beer to sustain him through long hours at the local blast furnace. Never having seen the film version of this masterpiece, I can only speculate as to what other horrors occurred in this now beerless town, but life without beer, or love, is no life at all.

Having spent my life in search of obscure references to beer, let me now offer you some of my favorite beer dialogue from the movies. Popcorn is optional — the beer is not.

"No tea, Mrs. Morgan. In training he is. A glass of beer if you please."

BARRY FITZGERALD IN "HOW GREEN WAS MY VALLEY," DIRECTED BY JOHN FORD, 1941

My word! is there anything better than English ale … let us thank God for simple pleasures, beef and beer!

"OF HUMAN BONDAGE," STARRING BETTE DAVIS AND LESLIE HOWARD, 1930S

Beer … "a high and mighty liquor"

JULIUS CAESAR

It's extraordinary how friendly you can make a lot of people on a couple bottles of beer.

BARON FRANKENSTEIN IN "FRANKENSTEIN," DIRECTED BY
JAMES WHALE, 1931

Wanna beer or somethin' like that? Wanna beer?
   Ok, sure.
What kind of beer would you like?
   What? I don't know. I don't care. Any kind.
I'll get you Rolling Rock, it's a good beer. It's the best around.

ROBERT DE NIRO TO MERYL STREEP IN "THE DEER
HUNTER," DIRECTED BY MICHAEL CIMINO, 1978

Perhaps the greatest beer lines ever uttered on the silver screen come from the 1941 Preston Sturges film "The Lady Eve" starring Henry Fonda and Barbara Stanwyck. The plot of this film has Stanwyck as a golddigging adventuress trying to swindle brewery heir Fonda out of his millions. Fonda, a simple soul who prefers snake hunting in the Amazon to living in society, is embarrassed by his family's beer business activities. Fonda's fortune comes from Pikes Pale —

The Ale that won for Yale. In a torrid love scene, Fonda delivers the following:

S: I thought you were in the beer business.

F: Beer! … Ale.

S: What's the difference?

F: Between beer and ale? … My father'd burst a blood vessel if he heard you say that. Beer's fermented on the bottom or maybe it's the other way around. There's no similarity at all. See, the trouble with being descended from a brewer, no matter how long ago he brewed it or whatever you call it, you're supposed to know all about something you don't give a hoot about. It's funny to be kneeling here at your feet talking about beer. You see, I don't like beer — Bock beer, Lager beer or Steam beer.

S: Don't you?

F: I do not. And I don't like Pale ale, Brown ale, Nut Brown ale, Porter or Stout which makes me gulp just to think about it. Wasn't enough to have everybody call me Hopsey ever since I was six years old …

BEER IN LITERATURE

*R*eferences to mankind's "oldest drink" are nearly as old as the written language itself. This is just a small, somewhat eclectic selection.

The servants who belong to thee
Come with the dinner things;
They are bringing beer of every kind, ...
Thou dost make him drink,
And then thou dost follow what he says ...
I am of a silent nature
And I do not tell what I see
I do not chatter.

TURIN PAPYRUS, ANCIENT EGYPT

I will make it felony
to drink small beer.
WILLIAM SHAKESPEARE,
KING HENRY VI

In the preparation of their beer they encroached very lavishly upon their corn-stores, quite indifferent to the fact that for the next two months they would be reduced to the necessity of grubbing after roots, and devouring any chance bird, or even any creeping thing, that might come their way.

Incredible quantities of legyee (beer) were consumed, so as to raise the party to a degree of excitement necessary for a prolonged revel.

SCHEINFURTH, HEART OF AFRICA, CIRCA 1870

> Doth it not show vilely in me to desire small beer?
>
> WILLIAM SHAKESPEARE,
> KING HENRY VI

Throw all the beer and spirits into the Irish Channel, the English Channel, and the North Sea for a year, and people in England would be infinitely better. It would certainly solve all the problems with which the philanthropists, the physicians, and the politicians have to deal.

SIR WILLIAM OSLER

If you couldn't afford good whiskey, he'd take you on trust for beer.

GERALD BRENNAN, FLORUIT,
SHANAHAN'S OULD SHEBEEN, 1899

"Did you ever taste beer?" "I had a sip of it once," said the small servant. "Here's a state of things!" cried Mr. Swiveller. ... "She *never* tasted it — it can't be tasted in a sip!"

CHARLES DICKENS (1812–1870),
NICHOLAS NICKLEBY

Mine host was full of ale and history.

RICHARD CORBET (1582-1653),
POEMS

"Bound in slavery –
Help him to be free

I'm hungry mother, why
does'nt father come Home?

And you say, said I, that the universe is really a vast pint of beer? . . . They proceeded with the speed of rockets to the northeast corner of the universe, which George now perceived to be shaped exactly like a pint of beer, in which the nebulae were the ascending bubbles.

JOHN COLLIER, THE DEVIL, GEORGE AND ROSIE *

Hermit hoar, in
solemn cell.
Wearing out life's
evening gray;
Strike thy bosom,
Sage! and tell
What is bliss, and
which the way?
Thus I spoke, and
speaking sigh'd
Scarce repress'd the
starting tear,
When the hoary Sage
reply'd,
"Come, my lad, and
drink some beer."

SAMUEL JOHNSON

Iago: She that could think and ne'er disclose her mind,
　　See suitors following and not look behind,
　　She was a wight, if ever such wight were, —
Desdemona: To do what?
Iago: To suckle fools and chronicle small beer.
Desdemona: O most lame and impotent conclusion!

WILLIAM SHAKESPEARE, OTHELLO, ACT I

Beer in the Kitchen

Be mine each morn with eager appetite
And hunger undissembled to repair
To friendly buttery; there on smoking crust
And foaming Ale to banquet unrestrained;
Material breakfeast! Thus in ancient days
Our ancesters robust with liberal cups
Usher'd the morn, unlike the squeamish sons
Of modern times.

PANEGYRIC ON OXFORD ALE, 1748

COLONIAL LIFE

Our drink has been beer and punch, made of rum and water: Our beer was mostly made of molasses, which well boyld, with sassafras or pine infused into it, makes very tolerable drink; but now they make mault, and mault drink begins to be common, especially at the ordinaries and the houses of the more substantial people. In our great town there is an able man, that has set up a large brew house, in order to furnish the people with good drink, both there and up and down the river.

WILLIAM PENN, WRITING AN ACCOUNT OF PROGRESS IN HIS COLONY, 1685

Of beer an enthusiast has said that it could never be bad, but that some brands might be better than others …

A.A. MILNE (1882–1956)

And many a skeleton shook his head.
'Instead of preaching forty year!,
My neighbour Parson Thirdly said,
"I wish I had stuck to pipes and beer."

THOMAS HARDY, CHANNEL FIRING, 1914

I think fourty-nine Guinnesses is piggish.

DYLAN THOMAS

At eve the day is to be praised; a woman after she is burnt; a sword after it is proved; a maid after she is married; ice after it has passed away; beer after it is drunk.

THE VIKING EDDA, 11TH CENTURY

We went into the bar-room, where the landlord and I discussed between us two bottles of strong ale, which he said were part of the last six which he had in his possession. At first he wished to drink sherry, but I begged him to do no such thing, ... The landlord allowed himself to be dissuaded, and, after a glass or two of ale, confessed that sherry was a sickly, disagreeable drink, ...

Of hard old ale ... according to my mind, is better than all the wine in the world.

GEORGE BORROW (1803–1881)

This miller hath so wisely bibbed ale,
That as an hors he snorteth in his slepe.

CHAUCER, CANTERBURY TALES

The job of filling tankards was not one that could be done in a hurry, for he liked them full, with just the right amount of head on them. I was not allowed to pour beer for the old man as one day I had joggled the barrel and had made the contents cloudy. This was, I think, the only sin which he had not forgiven me. Anything else was pardonable, but to make beer undrinkable was a very high blasphemy.

RUTHVEN TODD, 1946

If you ... want to take beer for the picnic or motor trip, resort to the old method of wrapping cold beer just out of the ice box in wet newspapers. It will stay cold for two hours.

VIRGINIA ELLIOTT, 1933

I have come to the conclusion that the Germans love beer ... The moment I crossed the frontier from wine-drinking France, I smelt hops, and I have smelt hops ever since ... go where you will, with the aroma from beer shops and breweries, and there is no denying the fact that the two great industries of the German nation are hop raising and beer drinking, the women attending to the former and the men to the latter.

In my innocence I once thought that beer drinking in England was carried to excess, but I was mistaken. Englishmen are in the infant class — in the ABC's — in acquiring a German's education in the practice of beer drinking.

HENRY RUGGLES, 1883

He went into an old taproom with a bare floor, spittoons, a pot-belly stove burning wood, and a droning congregation of old-timers drinking beer at the bar. He ordered a beer. An old man with white hair was there singing a song, holding a beer in one hand, waving his other hand with a firm, grave, completely un-selfconscious gesture of sincerity and pleased determination to sing. …Martin knew that some of these men had been drinking in this bar for almost half a century … drinking in this bar in the 1890's of New York when the beer wagons were drawn thundering over cobbles by massive horses. They had begun drinking here after their fathers, and their fathers had been drinking in this taproom in the 1840's of New York when the waterfront streets were over-spanned by jibbooms of ancient sailing ships. … He took off his hat and listened to the old man's song, and when it was over he bought the singer a beer and had it brought to him down the bar. They raised their glasses and drank to each other solemnly and respectfully across the room.

JACK KEROUAC, THE TOWN AND THE CITY, 1950

They who drink beer will think beer.

WASHINGTON IRVING
AND WILLIAM
WARBURTON
(1698–1779)

A long experience with clients has made me prefer a shabby whisky-drinker to a well-dressed beer-drinker.

GRAHAM GREENE (1904–1991)

Beer, of course, is actually a depressant, but poor people will never stop hoping otherwise.

KURT VONNEGUT, JR., HOCUS POCUS, 1990

Keep your libraries, keep your penal institutions, keep your insane asylums … give me beer. You think man needs rule, he needs beer. The world does not need your morals it needs beer. It does not need your lectures or your charity. The souls of men have been fed with indigestibles, but the soul could make use of beer.

HENRY MILLER (1891–1980)

He is not deserving the name of Englishman who speaketh against ale, that is, good ale.

GEORGE BORROW (1803–1881)

English lager, I must say, I have never liked.

GEORGE SAINTSBURY, 1920

[beer] is one of those commonplaces of life — those daily-expected and daily-enjoyed simple pleasures which give man's life its local colouring . . .In London it is our beer that stands foremost in

Without any doubt whatsoever this nectar was brewed in the waxing of the moon and of that barley which Brutus brought hither in the first founding of this land! And the water wherein that barley-corn was brewed was May-day dew, the dew upon the grass before the sunrise on a May-day morning. For it has all the seven qualities of ale, which are:

Aleph ... Clarity.

Beth ... Savour.

Gimel ... A lively hue.

Daleth ... Lightness.

He ... Profundity.

Vau ... Strength retained.

and lastly, Zayin, which is Perfection and The End. . . . It is indeed good beer; and when we leave our valleys we will all drink it together in paradise.

HILAIRE BELLOC (1870–1953), THE FOUR MEN

the ranks of pleasant thoughts ... Therefore it is that the cry of "beer" falls like music on the ear.

MR. WEIR, CIRCA 1800

When schoolboy friends meet once again, who
  have not met for years,
Say, over what will they sit down, and talk of
  their careers,

M.T. DWYER, President.   WH. H. FAY, Vice President.   P. J. FLYNN, Treasurer.   25

CRESCENT BREWING CO.

BREWERS AND BOTTLERS OF

Lager Beer, Ale & Porter.

ANNUAL CAPACITY 100,000 BARRELS.

Brewery at WALPOLE, N.H.   *Bellows Falls, Vt.* July 7 –1901
P.O. Address, BELLOWS FALLS, VT.

Sold to M. F. Dwyer and Co.

97	5/1	Ale			
	30/1	Lager			
	60/4	"			

Your "wishy washy" wines won't do, and fiery
   spirits fail,
For nothing blends the heart of friends like good
   old English ale.

J. CAXTON, CIRCA 1880

It was the most beautiful colour that the eye of an
artist in beer could desire; full in body, yet brisk
as a volcano; piquant, yet without a twang; lumi-
nous as an autumn sunset; free from streakiness

of taste; but, finally, rather heady. The masses worshipped it, the minor gentry loved it more than wine, and by the most illustrious country families it was not despised. Anybody brought up for being drunk and disorderly in the streets of its natal borough had only to prove that he was a stranger to the place and its liquor to be honourably dismissed by the magistrates as one overtaken in a fault that no man could guard against who entered the town unawares.

THOMAS HARDY, THE TRUMPET-MAJOR

A great deal of beer was brewed and drunk in Hoboken, but the consumption in the various beer halls was sedate and ruminative rather than boisterous.

Once a year — sturdy Protestants though they were — the brewers of Hoboken gave a great pre-Lenten ball (their Fasching, their Mardi Gras) in honor of King Gambrinus, the inventor of beer.

THORNTON WILDER, THE EIGHTH DAY

Back and side go bare, go bare,

Both foot and hand go cold;

But, belly, God send thee good ale enough,

Whether it be new or old.

BISHOP STILL, BISHOP OF BATH AND WELLS, 1551

The human stomach will easily accommodate numerous seidels of beer, poured in at regular or irregular intervals; but the human stomach cannot and will not take care of a similar number of seidels of water, or of any other liquid that comes in the guise of stuff that neither cheers nor inebriates. I have never looked up the scientific reason for this. I state it as a fact, proved by my own attempts to accomplish with water what I used easily to do with Pilsner and other naughty substances.

SAMUEL G. BLYTHE, THE OLD GAME, 1914

"And The Three Keys, is it still in existence?"

"Oh, it's there all right, but the brewers bought it when my uncle died and it's not a free house any more."

"Did they alter it much?"

"You'd hardly know it was the same house with all the pipes and tubes. They put in what they call pressure, so you can't get an honest bit of beer with-

*"Christmas morning in the **Drunkards Home**."*

Brehm asserts that the natives of Northeastern Africa catch the wild baboons by exposing vessels with strong beer, by which they are made drunk ... On the following morning they [the baboons] were very cross and dismal; they held their aching heads with both hands, and wore a most pitiable expression: when beer ... was offered them, they turned away with digust . . .

CHARLES DARWIN, THE ORIGIN OF SPECIES, 1859

out a bubble in it. My uncle was content to go down to the cellar for a barrel, but it's all machinery now."

GRAHAM GREENE, UNDER THE GARDEN, 1963

of course you'll have another drop [of ale]. A man's twice the man afterward. You feel so warm and glorious, ...

THOMAS HARDY, FAR FROM THE MADDING CROWD

How much beer is in German intelligence?

FRIEDRICH NIETZSCHE (1844-1900)

The first ... handed his neighbour the family mug — a huge vessel of brown ware having its upper edge worn away like a threshold by the rub of whole generations of thirsty lips that had gone the way of all flesh, and bearing the following inscription burnt upon its rotund side in yellow letters: there is no fun Untill i cum

THOMAS HARDY, THE THREE STRANGERS

I was offered beer first by Lubbock, my riding master, whom I visited one evening in summer. I hated the taste and drank it down with an effort to prove my manliness, and yet some days later, on a long country walk with Raymond, the memory of the taste came back to taunt my thirst. We stopped at an inn for bread and cheese, and I drank bitter for the second time and enjoyed the taste with a pleasure that has never failed me since.

GRAHAM GREENE

Come, my masters, I'll bring you to the best beer in Europe.

CHRISTOPHER MARLOWE

Of this strange drink, so like the Stygian lake,
Which men call ale, I know not what to make;
Men drink it thick and void it very thin,
Therefore much dregs must needs remain within.

HEYLIN, 1652

O ales that were creamy like lather!
O beers that were foamy like suds!
O fizz that I love like a father —
O fie on the drinks that are duds!

CHRISTOPHER MORLEY (1890–1957)

The saloon smells of brass polish and fresh saw-dust. Though an open window a streak of ruddy sunlight caresses the rump of a naked lady who reclines calm as a hardboiled egg on a bed of spinach in a giltframed picture behind the bar.

"Well Gus what's yer pleasure a foine cold mornin loike this?"

"I guess beer'll do, Mac."

The foam rises in the glass, trembles up, slops over. The barkeep cuts aross the top with a wooden scoop, lets the foam settle a second, then puts the glass under the faintly wheezing spigot again …

JOHN DOS PASSOS, 1925

If the home we never write to, and the oaths we
        never keep,
    and all we know most distant and most dear,
Across the snoring barrack-room return to break
        our sleep,
    can you blame us if we soak ourselves in beer?

RUDYARD KIPLING

There is no beverage which I have liked to live with more than Beer.

GEORGE SAINTSBURY, 1920

Why
Should I
Weep, wail, or sigh?
What if luck has
passed me by?
What if my hopes are
dead,
My pleasures fled?
Have I not still
My fill
Of right good cheer,
Cigars and beer?
GEORGE ARNOLD
(1834–1865)

The English working classes may be said to be soaked in beer. They are made dull and sodden by it. Children are … born to the smell and taste of it, and brought up in the midst of it.

JACK LONDON, 1903

Where you and I went down the lane with ale mugs in our hands …

G.K. CHESTERTON (1874–1936)

Visions of the old riotous evenings with the boys ran through his mind; a billiard table and the click of balls; the jolly conversation at the club, and glass after glass of that cold amber beer. The large freedom of the city streets at night, the warm saloons on every corner, the barrooms with their pyramids of bottles flashing in the gaslight — these were the things that made a man's life amusing.

CHRISTOPHER MORLEY

Pay-day came, and with it beer.

RUDYARD KIPLING

Come, hostess, dress it (a trout) presently, and get us what other meat the house will afford, and give us some of your best barley wine (strong ale), the good liquor that our honest forefathers did use to drink of; the drink which preserved their health, and made them live so long and do so many good deeds.

IZAAK WALTON, THE COMPLETE ANGLER (1593–1683)

Everyone hath a penny for the new Alehouse.

THOMAS FULLER, 1732

They told me this story, … while we were waiting for an up-train. I supplied the beer. The tale was cheap at a gallon and a half.

RUDYARD KIPLING (1865–1936)

Then we trotted gentle, not to break the bloomin' glass

   Though the Arabites 'ad all their ranges marked;

But we dursn't 'ardly gallop, for the most was bottled Bass,

An' we'd dreamed of it since we was disembarked.

RUDYARD KIPLING

Go now, like a dear, an' buy me a can, ... Jimmie took a tendered tin pail and seven pennies and departed. He passed into the side door of a saloon and went to the bar. Straining up on his toes, he raised the pail and pennies as high as his arms would let him. He saw two hands thrust down to take them. Directly the same hands let down the filled pail, and he left ...

STEPHEN CRANE, RUSHING THE GROWLER (1871–1900)

That it's beer for the young British soldier —
Beer, beer, beer, for the soldier.

RUDYARD KIPLING

Ere's to English women an' a quart of English beer.

RUDYARD KIPLING

And so, you see, 'twas beautiful ale, and I wished to value his kindness ... and not to be so ill-mannered as to drink only a thimbleful, which would have been insulting the man's generosity. And so I used to eat a lot of salt fish afore going, and then

by the time I got there I were as dry as a lime-bas-
ket so thorough dry that that ale would slip-ah,
twould slip down sweet! Happy times! Heavenly
times! Such lovely drunks as I used to have at
that house.

THOMAS HARDY (1890–1928)

Fill with mingled cream and amber
    I will drain that glass again.
Such hilarious visions clamber
    Through the chamber of my brain —

It was as natural as eating and to me as necessary, and I would not have thought of eating a meal without drinking ... Beer

ERNEST HEMINGWAY
(1899–1961)

Quaintest thoughts — queerest fancies
　Come to life and fade away:
What care I how time advances?
　I am drinking ale today.
　　　　　　EDGAR ALLAN POE (1809–49)

The curious "white ale" or lober agol — which, within the memory of man, used to exist in Devonshire and Cornwall ... was I believe, drunk quite new; but then it was not pure malt and not hopped at all, but had eggs ("pullet-sperm in the brewage") and other foreign bodies in it.

GEORGE SAINTSBURY, 1920

When the hour is nigh me,
Let me in a tavern die,
With a tankard by me.

— ARCHPOET, CONFESSIO, 12TH CENTURY

There's nothing as heartening as the sight of an empty pub in the morning, the shelves full and everything spick and span before the barbarian hordes come in. Them that drinks bottles spoil

the look of the shelves but draught is a different
story — you never see the barrel going down.

PATRICK McGINLEY

And brought of myghty ale a large quart.

CHAUCER